THE LIVES *and* LEGENDS *of the* DISCIPLES

12 WHO CHANGED *the* WORLD

MORRIS INCH

THOMAS NELSON PUBLISHERS, INC.
Nashville, Tennessee

Published in Nashville, Tennessee by Thomas Nelson, Inc.

Printed in the United States of America
1 2 3 4 5 — 07 06 05 04 03

Preface

Aristides, writing early in the 2nd century, observed: "These twelve disciples (apostles) went forth throughout parts of the world and continued to show His greatness with all modesty and uprightness." To appropriate an expression from Winston Churchill, "Seldom have so many been indebted to so few."

Who were these persons? What motivated them in their service? How are they remembered? These and related questions solicit our attention as we consider twelve who changed the world.

Critical to our understanding of the apostles is that they were called by Jesus to speak and act on His behalf. So it was that the early believers "continued steadfastly in the apostles' doctrine and fellowship" (Acts 2:42). It was a spiritual legacy they would pass down to succeeding generations.

For all practical purposes, the apostolic teaching encompasses the New Testament. The entries appear to have been written by the apostles or those associated with them. Consequently, it is proper to embrace them as normative for Christian faith and practice.

In another sense, the person is the message. We are encouraged to use our imagination to walk with the apostles along the dusty roads of antiquity. There we strain, along with them, to catch a glimpse of Jesus, and listen to His exciting words.

This book has been a cooperative task. Many thanks go to my editor, Angela Seres. Following much correspondence, we found clarification and a common understanding. I also thank her staff—Ramona Richards and Dan DePriest, and John Adams and Jennifer Zimmerman at ProtoType—who shaped it into its present form.

No doubt, we could have done better. I seldom review a text

without wishing I had done something differently. Then, too, it was not always easy to distinguish between a credible tradition and one lacking merit. After that, we labored over how to keep the discussion relatively simple, and not encumbered with uncertainties.

The book cover was, in itself, an artistic achievement. Thank you to Bill Chiaravalle and Barbara West for their efforts. Interestingly, the cover art, Rembrandt's *Storm on the Sea of Galilee,* was stolen from the Isabella Stewart Gardner Museum in Boston on St. Patrick's Day 1990. It was cut from the frame and rolled, leaving paint chips on the floor of the museum. Sadly, it was damaged. To date, this masterpiece has not been recovered.

Finally, may the apostles be with you in spirit. May they grace your life with the message conveyed, and in some measure embodied. As Paul earnestly wrote two millennia ago, "Grace be with all those who love our Lord Jesus Christ in sincerity" (Ephesians 6:24).

Morris Inch
December 2002

Table of Contents

Chapter One
The Shaliach

A man planted a vineyard and set a hedge around it, dug a place for the wine vat and built a tower. And he leased it to vinedressers and went into a far country. Now at vintage-time he sent a servant to the vinedressers, that he might receive some of the fruit of the vineyard from the vinedressers. And they took him and beat him and sent him away empty-handed. Again he sent them another servant, and at him they threw stones, wounded him in the head, and sent him away shamefully treated. And again he sent another, and him they killed; and many others, beating some and killing some. Therefore still having one son, his beloved, he also sent him to them last, saying, "They will respect my son." But those vinedressers said among themselves, "This is the heir. Come, let us kill him, and the inheritance will be ours." So they took him and killed him and cast him out of the vineyard. Therefore what will the owner of the vineyard do?

Mark 12:1–9

Jesus shared this parable of the wicked vinedressers with His disciples as a graphic illustration of the Shaliach tradition—a tradition that He and His twelve apostles would carry forth to change the world.

The Mishnah, the post-biblical compilation of Jewish law which, combined with the Gemara commentary, comprises the Talmud, reveals a passage that reads: "The one who is sent (Shaliach) is the same as the one who sends." Jesus draws His authority from His commission. Just as the vineyard owner conveyed power and authority to his messengers and ultimately to his own son to perform in the master's name, so did God convey power and authority to His Son to perform in His name. Jesus, in turn, conveyed this same power and authority to the twelve apostles. So, it is fitting that the term "apostle" derives from the Greek verb "to send."

All three synoptic Gospels—Matthew, Mark, and Luke—describe the commission of the twelve apostles. According to Mark's account: "And He went up on the mountain and called to Him those He Himself wanted. And they came to Him. Then He appointed twelve, that they might be with Him and that He might send them out to preach" (Mark 3:13–14). These were the twelve Jesus called:

- Simon Peter
- James of Zebedee
- John of Zebedee
- Andrew
- Philip
- Bartholomew
- Matthew, originally Levi
- Thomas
- James, son of Alphaeus

- Ω Jude Thaddaeus
- Ω Simon the Zealot
- Ω Judas Iscariot

Jesus summoned those He wanted, and by appointing His apostles, He transformed them from mere students who learned from Him, into messengers, that He might send them out to preach. In doing so, He also granted them authority to act on His behalf.

The apostles figured prominently in Jesus' public ministry. They became an inner circle of confidants, chosen at Jesus' discretion. Although they didn't appear to be out of the ordinary in any way, perhaps Jesus anticipated what they would become with the passing of time. With the exception of a few notable cases of rivalry, the apostles appear, not as competing, but complementary roles.

But, why twelve apostles? It begins with "the people of God as the people of the twelve tribes . . . the final form of the messianic community. In the calling of the Twelve, Jesus orders His work and theirs in accordance with the structure of redemptive history and its goal, the creation of the community of God."[1]

Following Judas' betrayal of Jesus and his subsequent suicide, the apostles numbered only eleven. Peter reminded the other apostles that their being with Jesus qualified them to speak from personal experience, and a replacement for Judas should be chosen accordingly. Matthias replaced Judas, and after the Ascension of Christ, Paul was also added. Paul admitted that he was "born out of due time" (1 Corinthians 15:8), meaning that Paul was not with Jesus from the beginning, but encountered Him following His Resurrection. Nonetheless, Paul had a special gift, and he was chosen for that purpose.

Although some scholars have maintained that only Paul was God's choice, both of these men were called by God. Matthias was chosen by lot from the group of disciples who had been with

Jesus following His baptism. The apostles' initiative for selecting a replacement would be consistent with their Shaliach authority. Appointment by lot was, in fact, to be considered a call by God. Paul, on the other hand, was a vehement crusader against Christ and His followers, and was on a journey to Damascus to hunt down Christians when he came face-to-face with his destiny.

When the day of Pentecost arrived, the believers were assembled together (Acts 2:1). Suddenly a sound like a blowing of a violent wind came from heaven, and filled the whole house where they were sitting. They saw what seemed to be tongues of fire that separated and came to rest on each of them. All were filled with the Holy Spirit, and began to speak in other tongues as the Spirit enabled them.

Amazed and perplexed, the pilgrims who had gathered for the religious festival asked one another, "Whatever could this mean?" (2:12). Some, however, made fun of them and accused them of having too much wine. But Peter, in his usual outspoken manner, rebuked them, "But this is what was spoken by the prophet Joel: 'And it shall come to pass in the last days, says God, That I will pour out of My Spirit on all flesh;'" (2:16–17).

Then, "they were dispersed throughout all the earth to preach the gospel as the Lord their Master had commanded them."[2] The apostles thus assumed the responsibility of writing the final chapter to salvation history. "I still have many things to say to you," Jesus had confided, "but you cannot bear them now. However, when He, the Spirit of truth, has come, He will guide you into all truth" (John 16:12–13). This promise seems especially meant for the apostles.

As for the larger fellowship, "they continued steadfastly in the apostles' doctrine and fellowship, in the breaking of bread, and in prayers" (Acts 2:42). Specific instructions were given, and the disciples diligently pursued the course set by the apostles.

The Shaliach

It remained for the apostles to foster the unity, purity, and universality said to characterize the fledgling community, even though they encountered many difficulties along the way. One such event occurred at the Jerusalem Council (Acts 15). Gentile converts were being fiercely criticized, and the apostles convened with the council elders to settle the matter. Again, it was Peter who spoke out. "God, who knows the heart," he observed, "acknowledged them by giving them the Holy Spirit, just as He did to us, and made no distinction between us and them, purifying their hearts by faith" (15:8–9). Their commonalities blurred any lines of distinction in regards to their faith.

The apostles shared many characteristics.

They were all commissioned for their undertaking, and spoke on behalf of the One who commissioned them—like the vineyard owner in Shaliach tradition.

They were twelve in number, symbolizing the people of God, plus one subsequently called the apostle to the Gentiles (Paul).

Allowing for this one exception, they were with Jesus from the beginning—His baptism by John. Special emphasis was given to being a witness to the Resurrection.

They were heralds of the kingdom of God and witnessed signs and wonders.

They presided over the community of faith, and ground its members in sound teaching.

Above all else, they set their goals high, and were prepared to reach those goals at any price.

Jesus instructed them to "make disciples of all the nations" (Matthew 28:19). He would no longer have them restrict their efforts to the Jewish people. It was time to reap among the Gentiles.

Charged with such an imposing task, they set out to fulfill their calling—each in some distinct manner. Following the Ascension, each carried their message in different directions and languages to the far reaches of the known world. Although their deaths made them martyrs, each died in a symbolically distinct manner. Jesus informed Peter, "Most assuredly, I say to you, when you were younger, you girded yourself and walked where you wished; but when you are old, you will stretch out your hands, and another will gird you and carry you where you do not wish" (John 21:18). He said this, according to John, to signify by what death Peter would glorify God.

The biblical perspective by which the apostles have been examined is carefully documented in Scripture. However, there is much to glean from the historical and traditional perspectives in regards to the apostles' personal lives and their individual missions. Examining the evidence, the symbols associated with, and the fulfillment of, their given names, and the ultimate result of their work on our lives today, can lead to a more thorough understanding of how the Shaliach tradition was played out in practice by the twelve apostles.

The third time Jesus showed Himself to His apostles after His death, He asked Peter three times if he loved Him, and three times Peter replied that he did. Following each of Peter's affirmations, Jesus told him, "Feed My lambs" (21:15), "Tend My sheep" (21:16), and "Feed My sheep" (21:17). Jesus tells Peter, "You follow Me" (21:22).

In the Shaliach tradition, Jesus gave instruction and authority to the apostles to feed the sustenance of salvation to His lambs of the world. He sent them, as heirs to the kingdom, out into the vineyard to collect for their Master, even if it ultimately ended their lives.

As earlier stated, the Mishnah reads, "The one who is sent (Shaliach) is the same as the one who sends." The Shaliach tradition is clearly seen in the parable of the wicked vinedressers. God sent many messengers to collect His due from the tenants of His vineyards, and they were all summarily rejected. Finally, He sent His own Son to speak for Him. The sinful tenants believed they could claim the inheritance outright by simply killing the Son, which they did.

Jesus asked, "Therefore what will the owner of the vineyard do? He will come and destroy the vinedressers, and give the vineyard to others" (Mark 12:9). Jesus gave the vineyard to the twelve apostles, so that they could give it to their disciples, not only as a map to salvation, but as the keys to the kingdom as well.

Jesus Christ was the first in the Shaliach tradition, and part of His Great Commission was to prepare the twelve apostles for their ultimate calling—to change the world.

With this in mind, let the journey begin.

Chapter Two
Simon Peter

Blessed are you, Simon Bar-Jonah, for flesh and blood has not revealed this to you, but My Father who is in heaven. And I also say to you that you are Peter, and on this rock I will build My church, and the gates of Hades shall not prevail against it. And I will give you the keys of the kingdom of heaven, and whatever you bind on earth will be bound in heaven, and whatever you loose on earth will be loosed in heaven."

Matthew 16:17–19

Peter originally came from Bethsaida and lived in Capernaum, which boasted plentiful springs and allowed for excellent irrigation. It was also the center of a vigorous fishing enterprise.

Galilee was a relatively affluent district at that time. It was said, "If you want to be wise, go south (to Judea), but if you want to be rich go north (to Galilee)." Then, too, Peter was no ordinary workingman. He and his partners owned fishing craft and the means to carry on a profitable business. Peter and his brother, Andrew, shared their fishing business with the brothers, James and John, sons of Zebedee (Luke 5:7, 10).

The district was referred to as Galilee of the Gentiles, since Greek cities were nearby and Gentile commerce took advantage of a branch of the Via Maris (Way of the Sea) trade route that worked its way through the Arbel Pass and along the northwestern shore of the Sea of Galilee. Capernaum straddled this route, attesting to its central location and providing a rationale for Jesus to select it as a base for His ministry.

Peter's brother, Andrew, was a disciple of John the Baptist, and was given to enlisting other disciples, so it was inevitable that Peter would be brought to Jesus (John 1:35–42).

The synoptic Gospels record an abbreviated version of Peter's meeting with Jesus (Matthew 4:18–20; Mark 1:16–18; Luke 5:1–11). "And Jesus, walking by the Sea of Galilee, saw two brothers, Simon called Peter, and Andrew his brother, casting a net into the sea; for they were fishermen. Then He said to them, 'Follow Me, and I will make you fishers of men'" (Matthew 4:18–20). In terms of time, they had much to lose. In terms of eternity, they had much to gain. They chose to follow Jesus.

Peter soon became an apostle chosen to minister specifically, but not exclusively, to Jews, as he was also a Jew. Of all the apostles,

Chapter Two

Peter was a man with whom modern men can most identify and even admire. He was an abrasive rebel and a bit of a loud mouth.

In the Acts of Peter and Andrew, a rich man of the city threatened the brothers. Peter responded by ordering a needle be brought to him. Then he saw a camel approaching. He ordered that the camel go through the eye of the needle. "Then the eye of the needle was opened like a gate, and the camel went through it, and all the multitude saw it." "Truly great is the God of Peter and Andrew," the man concluded, "and I from this time forth believe in the name of our Lord Jesus Christ."[3]

—*Legend*

Dr. Alexander Whyte, author of Bible Characters, summarizes Peter's personality most succinctly: "No disciple speaks so often and so much as Peter. Our Lord speaks oftener to Peter than to any other of His disciples: sometimes in praise, sometimes in blame. No disciple is so pointedly reproved by our Lord as Peter, and no disciple ever ventures to reprove his Master but Peter. No other disciple ever so boldly confessed and outspokenly acknowledged and encouraged our Lord as Peter repeatedly did, and no one ever intruded, and interfered, and tempted Him as repeatedly as Peter did.

Peter's Master spoke words of approval, and praise, and even blessing to Peter the like of which he never spoke to any other man. And at the same time, and almost in the same breath, He said harder things to Peter than He ever said to any other of His twelve disciples, unless it was to Judas."[4]

Peter certainly appears to be brash and impulsive. He is the first to speak, the first to act, and the last to think through the implications of his words or deeds. But despite all this, Jesus was patient with him. He knew that Peter's course was set, even if Peter himself did not yet know it. "Simon, Simon! Indeed, Satan has asked for you, that he may sift you as wheat. But I have prayed for you, that your faith should not fail; and when you have returned to Me, strengthen your brethren" (Luke 22:31–32). Jesus is telling him to stay the course that others will follow, even though it will be treacherous.

When Jesus instructed the apostles that the Son of Man must suffer many things, followed by execution and being raised from the dead, Peter naturally protested. In response, Jesus exclaimed, "Get behind Me, Satan! For you are not mindful of the things of God, but the things of men" (Mark 8:33). In this case, Peter may have been thinking exclusively in royal terms, as the Messiah was sometimes presented in royal garb, and would have easily discounted Jesus' passion. Thomas, on the other hand, maintained a completely contrary position when he said, "Let us also go, that we may die with him" (John 11:16). In the early days of Peter's discipleship, there were not many who would agree with him or come to his rescue.

Peter learned many lessons on his journey with Christ, and most of the time, he learned them the hard way. In one instance, Jesus met one of His followers on the road, and He explained to him that he couldn't purchase his passage to heaven with all of his riches. Jesus encouraged the man to sell all of his possessions, give the proceeds to the poor, and follow Him. The man was sad because he was very wealthy (Mark 10:17–22). When Jesus explained to His disciples the difficulties for a rich man to enter into the kingdom of heaven, Peter was the first to respond. "We have left all and followed you!" Peter exclaimed. "Assuredly, I say to you," Jesus solemnly replied, "there is no one who has left house or brothers or sisters or father or mother or wife or children or lands, for My sake and the gospel's, who shall not receive a hundredfold now in this time . . . and in the age to come, eternal life" (Mark 10:28–30). Eventually, Peter grew accustomed to being corrected by his Savior. It didn't take long before he learned to think before he spoke or acted on any emotional matter.

What is possibly the best known example of Peter's indecisively vacillating nature occurred when Jesus foretold the events that would follow His arrest. Peter said, "Even if all are made to stumble, yet I will not be" (14:29). Jesus then told Peter that he would, that very night, deny Him three times before the rooster crowed twice. Peter denied this charge vehemently and exclaimed, "If I have to die with You, I will not deny You!" (14:31). Of course, Peter did deny Jesus three times. The following day, when Peter remembered what Jesus had told him, and realized that it all came to pass exactly as Jesus had described, he was reduced to weeping. If genuine remorse is the key to recovery, then this moment marks the time in Peter's life when he put his foolishness away and began to act more responsibly. He was transformed from a lump of clay perpetually in a state of reshaping; to the rock that Jesus claimed he would be when He called him Cephas—a stone (John 1:42). After being put through the fiery kiln as a witness to his Savior's life, death, and Resurrection, Peter began to fulfill the meaning of his name, and in turn, began to live his life in the Shaliach tradition. He was singled out as one who denied his Lord, but was restored to favor and service by the death of the very One whom he denied.

The third time Jesus showed Himself to His apostles after His death and Resurrection, He asked Peter three times if he loved Him, and three times Peter replied that he did. Following each of Peter's affirmations, Jesus said to him, "Feed My lambs" (John 21:15), "Tend My sheep" (21:16), and "Feed My sheep" (21:17). Finally, Jesus told Peter, "You follow Me" (21:22). Peter's initial response may have been something short of unconditional love, suggesting he had come to realize how easily one waivers under pressure. Jesus appeared to be satisfied with Peter's realistic affirmation as a step in the right direction.

Despite Peter's remarkable ability to argue with Jesus, he also had a remarkable amount of faith in Jesus. During one particular incident, recounted in the Book of Matthew, Jesus and some of His disciples had gone to Capernaum, where Peter was asked if Jesus would be paying the temple tax. Peter said yes, and went to Jesus to discuss the matter. He sent Peter to the sea to cast a hook and catch a fish. In that fish's mouth, according to Jesus, would be the exact amount needed to pay the tax for Himself and for Peter (Matthew 17:24–27). At the sea, Peter caught the fish, and inside the mouth of that fish, was the coinage, just as Jesus instructed. The female tilapia fish, also known as St. Peter's fish, carries her babies in her mouth to protect them until they are old enough to care for themselves. They only vacate long enough for her to eat, and then they return. She is known for picking up shiny objects and holding them in her mouth to keep her babies from returning when it's time for them to venture forth on their own. This would account for the coins being inside the fish. As for the exact amount of coins, and the exact location where Peter would find the fish, Jesus must have had divine control over the event in order to show Peter how to believe.

Peter required a mix of love and admonishment another time when Jesus sent the apostles across the sea on a boat. During the journey, a great storm blew across the water. Peter, being somewhat of a retired fisherman, knew the danger of such a storm, and they were all afraid. Suddenly, they saw Jesus walking toward them on the water. At first, they thought they were seeing a ghost, but Jesus assured them that He was real and that they shouldn't be afraid. Naturally, it was Peter who had the boldness to speak. "Lord, if it is You, command me to come to You on the water" (Matthew 14:28). Jesus bade him to come, and Peter left the boat and began to walk on the water toward Him. But, when Peter saw the crashing waves and felt the stinging wind, he became afraid and lost his faith. He began to sink, and he cried out, "Lord, save me!" (14:30). Jesus stretched out His hand, caught Peter, and said, "O you of little faith, why did you doubt?" (14:31). When they returned to the boat, the sea was calmed. Peter wanted so much to be with his Savior, and to be like his Savior, that his faith gave him the courage to leave the safety of the boat. But, his faith waned in the face of adversity. And, true to form, Jesus not only rescued him, but reproved him for his floundering trust.

Peter had one final controversial moment with Jesus before He was arrested. Jesus knew that His death was imminent, and He wanted to show the apostles He loved so dearly one last display of His eternal servitude. He washed their feet. Peter would not allow this, exclaiming, "You shall never wash my feet!" But the Lord replied, "If I do not wash you, you have no part with me" (John 13:8). Peter, who still did not understand, insisted that if Jesus was going to wash his feet, then He should wash his hands and head, as well. Just when it seemed that Peter understood, something foolish came out of his mouth. But despite the obvious fact that his faith was slow in developing, Jesus loved him immensely.

Thereafter, several incidents are noted where Peter recognizes Jesus as the Son of God. In one particular instance, Jesus and His disciples went to the villages around Caesarea Philippi. On the way, He asked them, "Who do men say that I am?" They replied, "John the Baptist; but some say Elijah; and others, one of the prophets." "But who do you say that I am?" Jesus pressed them. Peter specifically answered, "You are the Christ" (Mark 8:27–29).

"Blessed are you, Simon Bar-Jonah," Jesus replied, "for flesh and blood has not revealed this to you, but My Father who is in heaven. And I also say to you that you are Peter, and on this rock I will build My church, and the gates of Hades shall not prevail against it. And I will give you the keys of the kingdom of heaven," Jesus continued, "and whatever you bind on earth will be bound in heaven, and whatever you loose on earth will be loosed in heaven" (Matthew 16:17–19).

In the tradition of the Shaliach, the technical terms "bind" and "loose" indicate the authority to lay down binding rules. Jesus was telling Peter that the student will become the teacher, and that his reward will be life everlasting in heaven.

In all of the synoptic Gospels, as the list of apostles unfolds, Peter is named first. This is not a coincidence, as his role became the most prominent. All four Gospels concur that Peter was, indeed, the leader of the apostles. In fact, he and the two sons of Zebedee (James and John) were part of an inner circle of trusted confidants to Jesus (Matthew 17:1; 26:37; Mark 5:37; 13:3). The last time Peter is mentioned in the biblical narrative with his brother, Andrew, is in Acts 1:13, when he and the other apostles retire to the Upper Room in Jerusalem following Jesus' Resurrection.

As the leader, Peter must have felt a great amount of responsibility for the care and future of the group, as a whole. After the death of Judas Iscariot, Peter inquired of his brethren, "Therefore, of these men who have accompanied us all the time that the Lord Jesus went in and out among us, beginning from the baptism of John to that day when He was taken up from us, one of these must become a witness with us of His resurrection" (Acts 1:21–22). Two men were then proposed—Joseph called Barsabas and Matthias. Matthias was chosen by lot to round out the twelve.

Chapter Two

In a resolute display of protectiveness, Peter took one of his first stands against a critical public. In the wake of Pentecost, when the Holy Spirit came upon the apostles and allowed them to speak in different languages, some of the witnesses accused the apostles of being drunk. Peter protested. "For these are not drunk, as you suppose . . . this is what was spoken by the prophet Joel: 'And it shall come to pass in the last days, says God, That I will pour out My Spirit on all flesh . . .' " (Acts 2:15–17). Peter continued, "Men of Israel, hear these words: Jesus of Nazareth, a Man attested by God to you by miracles, wonders, and signs which God did through Him in your midst, as you yourselves also know—Him, being delivered by the determined purpose and foreknowledge of God, you have taken by lawless hands, have crucified, and put to death: whom God raised up, having loosed the pains of death, because it was not possible that He should be held by it" (2:22–24). While not condoning their behavior, Peter allowed that God meant to bring good out of evil. This is also an incident where Peter seemed to offer a more merciful tone that was lacking in some of his previous exchanges.

Peter witnessed many astonishing miracles performed by Jesus. He was with Jesus when He healed the sick, the blind, and the lame—even raising people from death! Peter witnessed Jesus as He dramatically gave life back to Jairus' daughter (Mark 5:41–42). He was also present when Mary came to Jesus, weeping for her dead brother, Lazarus, who had been dead four days. Jesus was overcome with emotion, out of compassion for the anguish suffered by Mary and her sister, Martha, and also for His dear friend who had died. Jesus truly loved this family (John 11:5), so He went to Lazarus' tomb and called him out to live again (11:1–44). That must have been an indescribable scene for Peter.

He must have been most moved, however, by the miracle that took place in his own home (Mark 1:29–31). Peter's mother-in-law was in bed with fever. Jesus went to her, took her by the hand and helped her up. The fever left her, and she began to wait on them.

Another particular legend holds that Peter encountered the magician, Simon Magus, in Samaria. Simon was exposed as a false prophet and rebuked for trying to buy the Holy Spirit from Peter. So, Simon fled to Rome where he found favor with the emperor and established a profession involving every manner of heresy. Peter followed and found himself in contest with the magician. Simon claimed that he was a god and could raise one of the emperor's relatives from the dead. When he failed to do so, Peter, with the assistance of Paul, restored the youth to life. Apparently, this was just one of many instances where Simon the magician was humiliated by the apostles. Finally, the magician claimed that he would fly up to heaven with everyone, including the emperor, in attendance as witnesses. He climbed to the top of a tower, and flung himself into the air. It seemed that he hung in mid-air for awhile, until Peter, dropping to his knees, commanded the magician to be released. Simon Magus the magician fell to the ground, breaking his leg. The people, seeing that Simon was indeed nothing but a fraud, stoned him to death.

—*Legend*

Chapter Two

This would be an appropriate juncture to mention that there has been some dispute over the marital status of the apostles. It is interesting to note that when Peter left to follow Jesus, he appears to have remained a family man. After all, Jesus healed his mother-in-law in their home in Capernaum. Paul also mentions Peter's marital status in his first letter to the Corinthians. "Do we have no right to take along a believing wife, as do also the other apostles, the brothers of the Lord, and Cephas?" (1 Corinthians 9:5). Apparently, Peter was not the only married apostle, but he was named specifically in this verse. There is also a legend associated with Peter's wife claiming that she was martyred moments before her husband, and that he encouraged her to be faithful to Christ even unto death.

Scripture recalls countless activities of Peter prior to, and following, the death and Resurrection of Jesus Christ. Many of them involve miraculous healings and dramatic rescues. One such story involves Peter and John, who were on their way to the temple for afternoon prayer a short time after Jesus' death. A cripple was being carried to a temple gate called Beautiful, where he would beg each day. When the apostles came near him, he asked them for money. They looked at him and Peter said, "Silver and gold I do not have, but what I do have I give you. In the name of Jesus Christ of Nazareth, rise up and walk" (Acts 3:6). Peter took the man by the hand and brought him up where he was immediately healed. The three of them went into the temple together, and all who saw were amazed because they knew that the beggar had been lame. Peter responded to the people, "Men of Israel, why do you marvel at this?" (3:12). He assured them that this did not happen by their own power, but by that of the God of Jesus, and he reminded them that they were the people who put Jesus to death; ". . . faith in His name, has made this man strong, whom you see and know. Yes, the faith which comes through Him has given him this perfect soundness in the presence of you all" (3:16). But then, Peter softened by reiterating what Jesus said of His accusers while He was dying on the Cross, "I know that you did it in ignorance, as did also your rulers" (Acts 3:17). So, Peter gently urged them to repent and convert. Unfortunately, his charismatic speech landed him in prison with John by his side (Acts 4).

The following day, Peter and John were brought before a council of rulers, elders, and scribes and questioned about their actions regarding the lame beggar. "By what power or by what name have you done this?" (4:7) they asked. Then Peter, filled with the Holy Spirit, said to them, "If we this day are judged for a good deed done to a helpless man, by what means he has been made well, let it be known to you all . . . that by the name of Jesus Christ of Nazareth, whom you crucified, whom God raised from the dead, by Him this man stands here before you whole. This is the 'stone which was rejected by you builders, which has become the chief cornerstone'" (4:9–11). The council members were amazed that such a seemingly uneducated man could speak so eloquently and boldly, and realized that Peter and John had been followers of Jesus. Then, upon witnessing the healthy man who was once lame, they conferred amongst themselves and concluded that they must put an end to their healing and preaching, lest the proletariat would begin to follow them in the name of Jesus Christ.

They brought John and Peter before them again, and demanded that they stop spreading the Gospel of Jesus. After denying Jesus three times, Peter must have felt a powerful surge of redemption when he replied to them, "Whether it is right in the sight of God to listen to you more than to God, you judge. For we cannot but speak the things which we have seen and heard" (4:19–20). Peter was willing to die at that moment for his faith—not a bad turnabout for a man who went from tilting at windmills to having the faith of a child. Fortunately, his time to die for his faith wasn't for years to come.

Chapter Two

That child-like faith turned into sheer and terrifying strength when he faced Ananias and his wife, Sapphira. The couple had plotted to cheat God by keeping back a portion of the proceeds from an item they were to sell and donate to those in need. Peter asked Ananias, "Why has Satan filled your heart to lie to the Holy Spirit . . . While it remained, was it not your own? . . . You have not lied to men but to God" (Acts 5:3–4). Ananias died instantly, and when his wife arrived shortly thereafter and repeated the lie, she also died. The typical commentary about Ananias and Sapphira teaches that their giving was totally voluntary but tainted with deception, pride, and greed. Failing to give all did not condemn them. They were condemned when they attempted to deceive the Lord and the brethren by blessing themselves with the blessings of others.

The apostles performed many miraculous acts such as these, and the people were awestruck. After the incident involving Ananias and Sapphira, the sick were brought into the streets and laid on beds or mats in hopes that Peter's shadow might fall on them and cure them (5:15).

The council that warned Peter and John when they healed the lame beggar was not impressed, however. They called on them again, and reminded them that they had been forbidden to teach in the name of Jesus Christ. At this, Peter and the other apostles exclaimed, "We ought to obey God rather than men!" (5:29). The council wanted to put the apostles to death, but a Pharisee named Gamaliel urged them, "let them alone; for if this plan or this work is of men, it will come to nothing; but if it is of God, you cannot overthrow it—lest you even be found to fight against God" (5:38–39). Gamaliel was a teacher of the law and honored among the people. He was also the spiritual mentor of Saul of Tarsis, who would become the apostle Paul. Gamaliel's words persuaded them, and after they had the apostles flogged, they let them go. To the dismay of the council, the apostles continued their activity.

Simon Peter

There was a centurion named Cornelius. He and all his family were among those gentiles whom the Jews called God-fearers, because they worshiped the God of Abraham.

Probably the most beautiful and passionate legend surrounds Peter and his wife, Perpetua. According to 1 Corinthians 9:5, Perpetua, who may have been the daughter of Aristobulus, accompanied him during some of his travels. Her life in history was never made clear in Scripture, but there are several accounts of her death. In Edgar J. Goodspeed's book, *The Twelve,* he quotes from the accounts of Clement of Alexandria in his Miscellanies and from Eusebius in his Church History: "They say that when the blessed Peter saw his own wife led out to die, he rejoiced because of her summons and her return home, and called to her very encouragingly and comfortingly, addressing her by name, and saying, 'O thou, remember the Lord!'" Peter and his wife apparently were of one mind in regards to issues of faith, and they were both willing to give their lives, apart from one another or together, in order to serve their Lord.[5]

—*Legend*

He gave generously to those in need, and prayed to God regularly. On one occasion, an angel appeared to him. The angel told him to send men to Joppa to find the man named Simon who is called Peter and bring him back (Acts 10:4–5).

Chapter Two

Around noon the following day, Peter was praying on a rooftop when he became hungry. While his food was being prepared, Peter fell into a trance and saw a vision. He saw heaven opened, and something like a sheet being let down to the earth. It contained all kinds of creatures. "Rise, Peter," a voice urged him. "Kill and eat." "Not so, Lord!" Peter protested. "For I have never eaten anything common or unclean" (Acts 10:13–14). This happened three times, and the sheet was drawn back into heaven. While Peter was puzzling over the meaning of the vision, the Spirit prompted him, "Behold, three men are seeking you. Arise therefore, go down and go with them, doubting nothing; for I have sent them" (10:20). Peter welcomed the delegation from Cornelius, and the next day they started the return journey.

Cornelius had gathered his relatives and close friends in anticipation of Peter's arrival. Peter, remembering his vision, concluded, "In truth I perceive that God shows no partiality. But in every nation whoever fears Him and works righteousness is accepted by Him" (10:34–35). While he was still speaking, the Holy Spirit came upon those listening to him, and they were baptized.

Later, when Peter went to the Jerusalem Council, the circumcised believers denounced him by saying, "You went in to uncircumcised men and ate with them" (11:3). Peter shared with them the circumstances surrounding his acceptance of hospitality from Cornelius. After hearing Peter, the Jerusalem Council had nothing more to condemn and praised God saying, "Then God has also granted to the Gentiles repentance to life" (11:18).

But Peter's time was running short. Herod had arrested some of the believers. James, the brother of John, had been executed. While grandstanding for his minions, Herod had Peter captured and imprisoned, with the intention of further pleasing the masses. The night before the apostle was to be brought to trial, he "was sleeping, bound with two chains between two soldiers; and the guards before the door were keeping the prison" (Acts 12:6). Suddenly an angel appeared, and a light illuminated the cell. The angel told Peter to get up. His chains fell away. He passed the first and second guards, and when he came upon the iron gate leading to the city, it opened by itself. Once again, by the grace of God, Peter escaped death to continue his ministry. How he must have grieved over the death of his old friend, James. But his heart must have been so full knowing that the Lord desired for him to have a longer life in order to accomplish his missions.

Peter returned to the Jerusalem Council once more to speak on behalf of Gentile believers. Pharisees had spoken out harshly about the issue of circumcision, claiming that the procedure was necessary as dictated by the Law of Moses. There was a heated debate, and Peter spoke. "Men and brethren, you know that a good while ago God chose among us, that by my mouth the Gentiles should hear the word of the gospel and believe . . . God, who knows the heart, acknowledged them by giving them the Holy Spirit, just as He did to us, and made no distinction between us and them, purifying their hearts by faith. Now, therefore, why do you test God by putting a yoke on the neck of the disciples which neither our fathers nor we were able to bear?" (15:7–10). With these gentle, yet persuasive, words, Peter was able to urge the assembly not to unnecessarily burden the Gentile believers.

It was apparent that, although Peter had been appointed an apostle to minister to Jews, he was also instrumental in ministering to Gentiles.

But, Peter was not always on the good side of his brothers on every issue, as noted in one instance where Paul admonished Peter after a brief revisit of his seemingly retired vacillating nature. When Peter came to Antioch, Paul "withstood him to his face, because he was to be blamed" (Galatians 2:11). Apparently, Peter had no problem eating and socializing with Gentiles until "certain men" came along and Peter separated himself, fearing those who were circumcised. The other Jews joined Peter in practicing his hypocrisy. "But when I saw that they were not straightforward about the truth of the gospel," Paul elaborated, "I said to Peter before them all, 'If you, being a Jew, live in the manner of Gentiles and not as the Jews, why do you compel Gentiles to live as Jews?' " (Galatians 2:14). Paul succeeded in persuading Peter to follow a consistent course of action. Peter must have been so graciously thankful to Paul, his brother in Christ, for his guidance and wise words.

The Epistles of Peter

Peter may have authored both 1 and 2 Peter, objections notwithstanding—if not Peter, then likely one of his associates in the apostolic mission. Moreover, Mark is said to have drawn from Peter for his gospel narrative.

First Peter

First Peter was written around A.D. 64. The author identifies himself as "Peter, an apostle of Jesus Christ" (1 Peter 1:1). He acknowledges his recipients as churches in five Roman provinces throughout western Turkey; "To the pilgrims of the Dispersion in Pontus, Galatia, Cappadocia, Asia, and Bithynia" (1:1). "By Silvanus, our faithful brother as I consider him, I have written to you briefly, exhorting and testifying that this is the true grace of God in which you stand" (5:12).

Peter offered this letter as words of encouragement and strength for persecuted Christians. Rome did not consider Christianity as a part of Judaism, but rather as a cult. At the very least, the Romans did not understand Christian traditions. Christians were encouraged to greet one another with a "kiss of love" (1 Peter 5:14). Communion bread and wine represented the body and blood of Christ. It appeared to Romans that Christians were just a sect of incestuous cannibals. Rome, for the sake of stability, was severely persistent in its efforts to force Christians to conform to Roman beliefs. Punishment ranged from mere threats to execution.

With this opposition in mind, Peter sought to comfort Christians with words of encouragement. First, he implored his readers to be "as obedient children, not conforming yourselves to the former lusts, as in your ignorance; but as He who called you is holy, you also be holy in all your conduct" (1:14–15). Peter knew that, aside from the persecutions, there were many other spiritual obstacles standing between Christians and their daily walk of faith—namely the desire to disobey in the face of adversity. Peter told them, "For it is better, if it is the will of God, to suffer for doing good than for doing evil" (3:17). He assured them of their secure salvation in Christ, and quoted from the prophet Isaiah, saying, "All flesh is as grass, And all the glory of man as the flower of the grass. The grass withers, And its flower falls away, But the word of the Lord endures forever" (1:24–25).

Peter knew that their lives were difficult and they wanted to rebel against the unjust authority of Rome, but Peter encouraged them to be like Jesus—to serve and suffer in obedience to God, to resist retaliation, and to submit to all levels of authority in society. He used Jesus' suffering as an example and urged his readers to follow in Christ's footsteps by not retaliating.

Peter closed his letter with instructions to submit to one another, to be humble, sober, and vigilant. Lastly, Peter urged his readers to resist the devil who "walks about like a roaring lion, seeking whom he may devour" (5:8).

This first epistle was Peter's attempt to guide his flock, in shepherd fashion, in the ways of God.

Chapter Two

Second Peter

Second Peter was written around A.D. 65. The author identified himself as "Simon Peter, a bondservant and apostle of Jesus Christ" (2 Peter 1:1). Peter's second letter served a dual purpose. First, he denounced false teachers of a distorted gospel, and warned about the dangers of believing them. Second, he explained the promise of the return of Christ.

Once again, in shepherd fashion, Peter attempted to keep the flock together and warned them against the dangers of being led astray by false teachers who have come into their communities. Peter said they have "eyes full of adultery and that cannot cease from sin, enticing unstable souls. They have a heart trained in covetous practices" (2:14). Peter called them "presumptuous," "self-willed," and insisted that they "will utterly perish in their own corruption" (2:10, 12).

His passion is clearly evident when he described the environment in which these false teachers operate: "These are wells without water, clouds carried by a tempest, for whom is reserved the blackness of darkness forever. For when they speak great swelling words of emptiness, they allure through the lusts of the flesh, through lewdness, the ones who have actually escaped from those who live in error" (2:17–18).

Then, Peter directed his attention to Christians who have begun to lose faith while waiting for the fulfillment of the promise that Christ would return. Peter responded with a succinct, yet extremely tender statement: "But, beloved, do not forget this one thing, that with the Lord one day is as a thousand years, and a thousand years as one day" (3:8). Peter told his readers that the wait is necessary in order that all people will come to Christ, and that no one will be left behind. And he told them that they should be vigilant because "the day of the Lord will come as a thief in the night" (2 Peter 3:10).

In closing, he told his readers to "grow in the grace and knowledge of our Lord and Savior Jesus Christ" (3:18).

One interesting aspect of this second letter is Peter's foreboding of his own death. "Yes, I think it is right, as long as I am in this tent, to stir you up by reminding you, knowing that shortly I must put off my tent, just as our Lord Jesus Christ showed me. Moreover I will be careful to ensure that you always have a reminder of these things after my decease" (1:13–15). Peter made it clear that, as long as he had breath in his body, he would continue to shepherd the flock, to deliver the message, and to proclaim the teachings of Christ. But, he received word that he would die soon. Despite this foreboding, he promised to continue to care for his sheep even after his death.

The Book of Mark

The author of Mark is not identified, but it is believed that John Mark wrote it while in Italy between A.D. 62 and 63, and is based on the memories of Peter. John Mark may not have met Jesus, but he was very familiar with Peter. Peter went to the home of John Mark's mother when he was released from prison by the angel (Acts 12:12). Peter and John Mark may have spent time together in Rome during the Christian persecutions in the early 60s, and as a result, their experiences through that trauma would have invariably resulted in a very strong bond between them.

Mark began with John the Baptist preaching in the desert, and ended with Jesus appearing to the eleven after His Resurrection and before ascending to heaven. The story moves in a fast-paced manner while describing how Jesus chose his "fishers of men" followed by the casting out of a demon in Capernaum. He continues with Jesus' parable of the sower, the healing of a woman who touched Jesus' robe, and then Jesus feeding 5,000 people with five pieces of bread and a few fish. Mark's account covers the event of Peter confessing his faith and Jesus then telling His disciples that the Son of Man will suffer, be killed, and will rise again. Sick at the prospect of his Lord suffering, Peter attempts to silence Him when Jesus says, "Get behind Me, Satan! For you are not mindful of the things of God, but the things of men" (Mark 8:33).

Mark is similar in content to the other two synoptic Gospels, but focuses more squarely on the activities of Jesus and His apostles, rather than the actual teachings and lessons.

Mark's account wrestles with the greatest life ever lived, according to the memories of his close ally, Peter. Peter must have doggedly followed Jesus toward Jerusalem, all the while recalling his days laboring as a fisherman and how he came to his itinerant ministry, curled up under a tree when no home was open to him; the questions that must have tormented his sleepless moments.

What Jesus Saw and Loved in Peter

Today, Peter would be considered the consummate type "A" personality in the areas of both weaknesses and strengths. His leadership of the other disciples from the beginning was legitimized by his initiating temperament and the Lord's own encouragement. His bull-headedness, however, often earned him rebuke and correction (Matthew 16:21–23; John 13:6–10; Galatians 2:14). Jesus saw in Peter the image of God's strength and God's calling for him to be the chief servant and first piece of stone (petros) from the rock (Petra) (John 1:42). The Lord bequeathed to all the apostles the same kingdom authority (Matthew 18:18), but it was to Peter that this authority was given first on the night of his confession of Christ 16:18). That Jesus understood Peter's aggressive and controlling nature and also his potential is seen in the numerous ways He deftly restrained, redirected, and rebuked Peter without destroying his strength. What Peter needed most was time with Jesus to replace the arrogance, fear, and control over his own agenda with faith, love, and hope in Christ alone.

Paul demonstrated his understanding of true leadership, not by pressuring the Gentiles to follow him and his agenda, but by pointing to the One whom he followed (1 Corinthians 11:1). Similarly Joshua led Israel by declaring his choice to serve the Lord, even if alone. Near the end of His time, the Lord sent Peter and the others out in pairs to preach and work miracles. Instead of returning with an arrogance and plans for improving their effectiveness, as he likely would have sometime earlier, he had been strengthened in the ways that mattered enough for the Father to open his eyes to see truth and his mouth to speak it. He didn't glorify his own strength but the Lord's. He had not yet fully laid down his own agenda as seen later when he rebuked Jesus for talking about His sufferings and death (Mark 8:32), but Jesus could then encourage him with recognition that he was leading in the spirit of Joshua.

It wouldn't be until Pentecost that Peter would speak out of the Lord's Spirit alone. Thus even in the final struggle with Peter, Jesus followed His rebuke concerning Peter's eminent denial of Him with the assurance that He had prayed further strength for him against Satan. Then Jesus reminded Peter to pass the Spirit's strength on to his brothers. The Lord even showed him how, when He, being God, took the lowest possible servanthood by washing the resistant Peter's feet. Jesus, however, had to rebuke Peter's presumption once again by showing him what it means to have a part with Him. If he is to be petros, a part with Him (John 13:8), he must do as the chief servant does. The Shaliach tradition calls a true leader to accept the mantle of humble, not glorified, service by his receiving humble service from his Lord. Peter's understanding of and faithfulness to this grace grew stronger as he served those he shepherded.

The Lord's calling for Peter in particular was to fulfill it out of his love for Him (John 21:15–23) and not out of the fear and arrogance that controlled him and made him controlling. Peter's greatest triumph was that, by the Spirit of Christ, he conquered himself.

The Death of the Apostle Peter

Prior to his death, Peter traveled extensively and took the gospel to many areas of Asia Minor. He wrote his first epistle to the Christians of Pontus, Galatia, Cappadocia, Asia, and Bithynia—all places he visited. He also traveled to Corinth, Greece, and Antioch, which is now Syria. There may be some evidence that he traveled through Gaul and Britain, as well.

The last days of Peter's life were spent in Rome. Apparently, he had visited Rome many times during his ministry. Reports indicate that Peter was imprisoned in The Mamertime, the infamously horrible dungeon and torture chamber located in Rome. Mamertime claimed the lives of thousands of Christians during Rome's persecutions. Peter survived for nine months, chained to a column and unable to lie down, but his spirit was not broken. In *The Drama of the Lost Disciples,* George F. Jowett writes, "(Peter's) magnificent spirit remained undaunted. It flamed with the immortal fervour of his noble soul proclaiming the Glory of God, through His Son, Jesus Christ . . . In spite of all the suffering Peter was subjected to, he converted his gaolers, Processus, Martinianus, and forty-seven others . . . Peter, the Rock, as he predicted, met his death at . . . the hands of the murderous Romans, who crucified him . . . Peter demanded to be crucified in the reverse position, with his head hanging downward. Ironically enough, this wish was gratified by the taunting Romans in Nero's circus A.D. 67."[6]

Most references concerning Peter's demise are brief and to the point. For instance, Peter of Alexandria writes: "Peter, the first of the apostles, was often arrested, thrown into prison, and treated with dishonor. He was finally crucified in Rome."[7]

A more extended account of the apostle's execution suggests that when Peter was crucified, he said, "Since my Lord Jesus Christ, who came down from the heaven upon the earth, was raised upon the cross upright, and He has deigned to call to heaven me, who am of the earth, my cross ought to be fixed head downmost, so as to direct my feet towards heaven; for I am not worthy to be crucified like my Lord."[4] This may have been Peter's final effort to atone for his denial of Jesus many years earlier.

The multitude that was assembled reviled Caesar, wanting to kill him. But Peter restrained them, saying, "A few days ago, being exhorted by the brethren, I was going away; and my Lord Jesus Christ met me, and having adored Him I said, 'Lord, where are you going?' And he said to me, 'I am going to Rome to be crucified.' And I said to him, 'Lord, were you not crucified once for all?' And the Lord answering said, 'I saw you fleeing from death, and I wish to be crucified instead of you.' And I said, 'Lord, I go; I fulfill your command.' And He said to me, 'Fear not, for I am with you.' Having thus spoken, he breathed his last.

According to Dorman Newman, in *The Lives and Deaths of the Holy Apostles,* Peter was embalmed by Marcellinus the Presbyter, then buried in the Vatican near the Triumphal Way. It was then removed to a cemetery in the Appian Way a few miles from Rome until the reign of Constantine, who had the body returned after rebuilding and enlarging the Vatican in honor of St. Peter.[8]

His head is reportedly entombed in a bust of silver in the Cathedral of St. John Lateran in Rome.

In June of 1968, Pope Paul VI announced that the bones of St. Peter had been found and were indeed beneath the basilica of St. Peter's in Rome.

Chapter Two

The Name of Peter

There are actually four forms of Simon Peter's name recorded. The Hebrew/Greek Simeon/Simon and the Aramaic/Greek Cephas/Petros. His given name was Simon Bar-Jonah, or Simon, the son of John. Simon was probably an alternative name, rather than an equivalent to Peter, simply reflecting the bilingual character of the region.

When Jesus met Peter, he observed, "You are Simon the son of Jonah. You shall be called Cephas" (John 1:42). Cephas, when translated, is Peter. John's account abruptly stops at this point, and if this brief narrative had been the only indication, it would appear that Peter had a relatively insignificant role as an apostle. However, as sometimes said, "Great things can have small beginnings."

At first, there doesn't appear to be any significance in the name Jesus gives to Peter. But later, he indeed fulfills the definition of his name upon his confession of Jesus as the Messiah.

By so naming Peter, Jesus was, in essence, telling him that he was a lump of soft clay, being shaped and molded to whatever situation presented itself, but that Peter would be put through the fire while journeying with Him, and would be forged hard as stone, never to be broken and never to be moved from his faith.

When Jesus said to Peter, "And I also say to you that you are Peter, and on this rock I will build My church, and the gates of Hades shall not prevail against it" (Matthew 16:18), Jesus was not talking about a geographical place where He wanted a church built. He was talking about an everlasting temple in Peter himself, and preparing him for his role as a leader in the early church. Peter was recognized as the first pope by the Roman Catholic Church.

(The Roman Catholic Church regards this text as the foundation of Papal succession. Peter thus becomes the foundation of the Lord's Holy Church and the Papacy is custodian of that apostolic authority. Most Protestant and especially evangelical scholars teach that it is not Peter the Lord was establishing here but the truth proclaimed by an inspired Peter that the Lord was not only Messiah but the Son of God. This foundation stone truth [rendered "petra" in Matthew 16:18] was Peter's testimony and would be the church's as well. Though textual support for the divinity of the Messiah can be offered from the Old Testament, the Jews couldn't seem to reconcile this with the certain knowledge of his humanity as descending from David. It had become standard by Peter's day to regard the Messiah as a divinely elevated man blessed from the womb above all men to deliver Israel to everlasting peace and glory. Yet Jesus now rejoiced to affirm Peter for being inspired. The Lord could now reveal that He would raise up a church, that it would be His alone, that it would be founded upon His life, death and Resurrection, and it would begin with Peter's testimony. As it turned out, it was Peter's words which gave birth to the church when three thousand souls believed on Pentecost.)

Apostolic Symbols and Patronages of Simon Peter

Peter is symbolized by a man holding a set of keys. This stands for Jesus' words to him about the "keys to the kingdom." Another symbol is that of a cock near his figure, symbolizing the crowing of the cock after he denied Jesus three times.

Peter's patronage is linked to:

- Bakers
- Bridge builders
- Clock makers, watch makers
- Cobblers, shoemakers, foot problems
- Fishermen
- Harvesters

- Locksmiths
- Longevity
- Masons
- Net makers
- Shipbuilders

Memorials

29 June (Feast of Peter and Paul)
22 February (Feast of the Chair of Peter)
18 November (Feast of the Dedication of the Basilicas of Peter and Paul)

Where to Find Peter in the Bible[9]

Before his call:

Matthew 16:17, John 21:15	Simon Barjona
Matthew 4:18	Brother of Andrew
Mark 1:30, 1 Corinthians 9:5	Married man
Acts 4:13	Not highly educated
Matthew 4:18	Fisherman

From his call to Pentecost:

John 1:40–42	Brought to Jesus by Andrew
John 1:42	Named Cephas by Christ
Matthew 4:18–22	Called to discipleship by Christ
Matthew 8:14, 15	Mother-in-law healed
Matthew 10:2–4	Called as an apostle
Matthew 14:28–33	Walks on water
Matthew 16:13–19	Confessed Christ's deity
Matthew 16:21–23	Rebuked by Jesus

Simon Peter

Ω Matthew 17:1–8, 2 Peter 1:16–18	Witnesses transfiguration
Ω Matthew 18:21	Asked important questions
Ω John 13:6–10	Refused Christ's menial service
Ω John 18:10, 11	Cuts off high priest's slave's ear
Ω Matthew 26:69–75	Denied Christ three times
Ω Matthew 26:75	Wept bitterly
Ω John 20:1–8	Ran to Christ's sepulcher
Ω John 21:1–14	Returned to fishing
Ω Matthew 28:16–20	Witnessed Christ's Ascension
Ω Acts 1:12–14	Returned to Jerusalem
Ω Acts 1:15–26	Led disciples

From Pentecost onward:

Ω Acts 2:1–41	Explained Spirit's coming at Pentecost
Ω Acts 3:1–11	Healed lame man
Ω Acts 5:1–11	Pronounces judgment
Ω Acts 5:14–16	Heals
Ω Acts 9:26, Galatians 1:17, 18	Met Paul
Ω Acts 9:36–43	Raises Dorcas
Ω Acts 10:1–23	Called to Gentiles
Ω Acts 10:24–46	Preached the gospel to Gentiles
Ω Acts 11:1–18	Explained his action to apostles
Ω Acts 12:3–19	Imprisoned—delivered
Ω Acts 15:7–14	Attends Jerusalem Council
Ω Galatians 2:14	Rebuked by Paul for inconsistency
Ω 2 Peter 3:15, 16	Commended Paul's writings

Chapter Two

Contrasts before and after Pentecost:

Ω Matthew 26:58, 69–74	Once coward, now courageous
Ω John 18:10	Once impulsive, now humble
Ω Matthew 16:21, 22	Once ignorant, now enlightened
Ω John 21:21, 22	Once deeply inquisitive, now submissive
Ω Matthew 26:33, 34	Once boastful of self, now boastful of Christ
Ω Matthew 14:28–31	Once timid and afraid, now fearless

Other related mentions:

Ω Matthew 17:24–27	Often the representative for the others
Ω John 21:15–19	Only disciple personally restored by the Lord
Ω Acts 3:12–26	Leader in the early church

From 1 Peter:

Ω 1:3–12	God's salvation
Ω 1:13–23	Obedience and holiness
Ω 2:4–6	Christ the corner stone
Ω 2:9	A royal priesthood
Ω 2:18–25	Christ's example
Ω 3:1–7	Husbands and wives
Ω 4:12–19	Partakers of His suffering
Ω 5:6–10	Be humble before God

From 2 Peter:

Ω 1:1–4	Things pertaining to life
Ω 1:5–11	Diligent growth
Ω 2:1–22	False teachers
Ω 3:9, 10	The hope of the day

Chapter Three
James of Zebedee

And when His disciples James and John saw this, they said, "Lord, do You want us to command fire to come down from heaven and consume them, just as Elijah did?" But He turned and rebuked them, and said, "You do not know what manner of spirit you are of. For the Son of Man did not come to destroy men's lives but to save them."

Luke 9:54–56

Now about that time Herod the king stretched out his hand to harass some from the church. Then he killed James the brother of John with the sword.

Acts 12:1–2

The only place in the New Testament where James Bar Zebedee is given exclusive attention is in Acts 12:2. There, he becomes the first of the twelve to suffer martyrdom and the only apostle whose death is recorded in the New Testament. Even here, he is identified as John's brother so as not to confuse him with James the Less, or even James, the Lord's brother (assuming the latter two are different). Nevertheless, we know a great deal about John's brother from his many appearances in the Gospels as one of the honored three whom Jesus purposely chose to be nearest Him.

In all instances, James is mentioned before John, so we can assume that he was the older brother and probably the first born of Zebedee. James is the English rendering of the Hebrew Ya'akov or Jacob, which means supplanter or usurper. The name finds earlier fulfillment in the scheming life of the Hebrew patriarch and son of Isaac.

The first son of Zebedee was no less deserving of the name, for we can see some of his self-promoting manner when he seeks the same place in the Lord's kingdom that he may have enjoyed at the Lord's table (Matthew 20:21; Mark 10:37). In like manner, he presumed to command fiery judgment upon the inhospitable Samaritans when he asked, "Lord, do you want us to command fire to come down from heaven and consume them, just as Elijah did?" (Luke 9:54).

James and John were fishermen with their father and partners with fellow apostles, Simon and Andrew. The Gospels do not say that Simon and Andrew left their father, Jonah. All we know for sure about James, in this regard, is that when Jesus called them both, he and John left their father and an unfinished day's work immediately.

Their mother, Salome, perhaps a fishing widow who obviously

adored her sons, joined them as a follower of Jesus, but Zebedee is not mentioned again. Zebedee is evidently prominent having other employees and presumably having some welcome in the high priest's home (Mark 1:20; John 18:16), and he may have still been alive when James was martyred some fifteen years later. If so, he would have had numerous opportunities to witness or hear of the signs and wonders which the apostles frequently performed in the Lord's name.

> For some years of his apostleship, James was in Spain and particularly the Iberian Peninsula before returning to Jerusalem and eventual martyrdom at the command of Herod Agrippa.
>
> —*Legend*

Jesus gave to the brothers the name "Boanerges," which means "Sons of Thunder" (Mark 3:17) because, in all probability, they both were of an aggressive and self-assertive nature. Evidence of this includes the two episodes already mentioned that were both followed by rebuke from Jesus.

Along with Peter, they were favored to be present at the miraculous fish catch, the healing of Peter's mother-in-law, the Transfiguration, the resurrection of Jairus' daughter, and the Lord's suffering at Gethsemane. For this, commentators often refer to Peter, James, and John as the "inner circle" of the Lord's disciples. Since we know that Peter was no milquetoast of a man, one might hastily theorize that Jesus prefers leadership for those He must restrain rather than those He must motivate. Or perhaps He kept them closer because their egos and aggressiveness needed more discipling to make them fruitful for Him, rather than for themselves. Why this inner circle was chosen is likely a much deeper matter.

In any case, the trio of Peter, James, and John appear from time to time in the biblical narrative as privileged confidantes to Jesus. For instance, "He permitted no one to follow Him except Peter, James, and John the brother of James" (Mark 5:37). When they came to the house of Jairus, the synagogue ruler, Jesus saw a commotion—people crying and wailing over the death of a child. "Why make this commotion and weep?" He inquired. "The child is not dead, but sleeping." They laughed at Him. After putting them all out, He took the child's parents and the trio with Him, and went to where the child lay. Jesus took her by the hand, and said to her: "Little girl, I say to you, arise!" The child obeyed and arose hungry as if from a long sleep. Those present were astonished. Jesus charged them not to tell anyone about what had happened (5:39–42). One wonders how Simon and the proud Sons of Thunder had the wherewithal to keep silent about it. Of course, after such a spectacular miracle, they may have been rendered absolutely speechless!

The same three also appeared with Jesus at His Transfiguration. Jesus led them up a high mountain by themselves (Matthew 17:1). Moses and Elijah soon joined them. Simon boldly presumed to offer a recommendation that they build three separate altars for them. At this, a voice from heaven exhorted the three to hear and venerate Jesus alone (vv. 5–8).

When they came down from the mountain, a man approached Jesus and knelt before Him. "Lord," he implored, "have mercy on my son, for he is an epileptic and suffers severely . . . I brought him to Your disciples, but they could not cure him." "O faithless and perverse generation," Jesus replied, "how long shall I be with you?" Then He rebuked a demon from the lad and he was healed. "Why could we not cast it out?" the disciples asked Him. He responded, "Because of your unbelief" (17:14–20). This event took on special significance for those who had been with Jesus on the mountain.

Concerning their rumblings that a Sadducee village needed burning, the Sons of Thunder may have had in mind an incident concerning Elijah. "Man of God," the king's emissary commanded him "Come down!" Elijah answered him, "If I am a man of God then let fire come down from heaven and consume you and your fifty men!" (2 Kings 1:9–10). Then fire fell from heaven and consumed the captain and his men. Thus, His calling was validated. In any case, Jesus rebuked His disciples. It was not His intent to destroy, but deliver those who had lost their way.

A reliable legend has it that the accuser named Josias, who served Herod's purposes in condemning James, was so moved by James' courage and devotion to Christ that he fell down in repentance at James' feet. James reached out to Josias, receiving him as a brother and they went together to the executioner's sword.

—*Legend*

The second thunder peal concerns a request made by the mother of Zebedee's sons. She came to Jesus and knelt down before Him. "What do you wish?" He inquired. She replied, "Grant that these two sons of mine may sit, one on Your right hand and the other on the left, in Your kingdom" (Matthew 20:21).

Salome may have expected that Jesus would honor her sons in the same way they had been in other areas of their lives. "The usual arrangement at a formal meal was to have a series of couches arranged in a U around the table. The guests reclined with their heads toward the table and their feet stretched out obliquely away from it. They leaned on the left elbow, which meant that the right hand was free to secure food."[10] The right hand seat was most honored because first, the host would be facing to the right, and secondly, in the reclining position, the "right hand man" would be nearest to the ear of the host. In eastern cultures, honor was the equivalent of love. The "seat of honor" or the seat of "the one most loved" are ancient expressions identifying one who was closest to a host at a table or most trusted by a monarch.

Even today, the clerk of a civil court will usually be seated at the right of the judge. The heir or prime minister of a king will usually be found standing to the right of the throne when court is held. Naval protocol will usually have the first mate or executive officer positioned at the table or at command to the captain's right.

Because their father was a noteworthy businessman, James, John, and their mother may have witnessed him being honored this way at noble banquets. Further evidence of their high social standing is the fact that John was known to the high priest and welcome in his home (John 18:16). Thus they may have come to anticipate prominence as their own unique inheritance, even as it extended into the Lord's kingdom.

Salome's request thus seemed natural and acceptable. It, "however, reflects the distorted perspective of human fallenness, wherein the greatest good appears to be that which serves the self, i.e., honor, position, glory, and prestige. It is the perspective that dominates the pagan world and its powerful rulers. The kingdom brought by Jesus defines greatness . . . in terms of servanthood."[11]

In answer to her request, Jesus was quick to associate the highest honors with the greatest sacrifices when He inquired directly of James and John their willingness to suffer as He would. "You do not know what you ask," Jesus said to them (including her sons). "Are you able to drink the cup I am about to drink?" "We are able," the brothers replied. "You will indeed drink My cup," Jesus allowed, "but to sit on My right hand and on My left is not Mine to give. But it is for those for whom it is prepared by My Father" (Matthew 20:22–24). The side lesson to us about sacrifice and rewards in this passage has its last word when Jesus reminds the willing sons of Zebedee, and us, that the Father alone possesses sovereignty to honor or dishonor whomever He will.

Jesus had desired to eat a final meal with His disciples. As they were reclining at the table, Jesus was troubled and said: "Most assuredly, I say to you, one of you will betray Me" (John 13:21). His disciples stared at one another, at a loss to know which of them He meant. One of them, the disciple Jesus loved, was reclining next to Him. Peter motioned to the disciple to ask about whom Jesus was referring. Leaning back against Jesus, he asked Him, "Lord, who is it?" Jesus replied, "It is he to whom I shall give this piece of bread when I have dipped it" (13:25–26).

Peter's location at the table is not identified, but if he had been to the left of Jesus, he could have inquired for himself and certainly motioning to John from there would have been very cumbersome. Therefore, it is likely that Peter was to John's right, which would be the third place of honor. Thus, if James and John were a stereophonic thunderclap at the Lord's right and left during well-provided meals, they may have expected the same places of honor in the Lord's kingdom.

It might seem, too, that Salome would take these kingdom honors for granted if both of her sons were already so seated as disciples. If, perhaps, James was not at the left shoulder of Jesus, he and his mother may have felt he should be, since he was the first born, after all, and one of the inner circle.

Some have supposed that Judas Iscariot was at the left hand of Jesus, since Jesus handed him the piece of bread that the King James Bible renders "the sop" (13:26). Their view that Judas, unlike

Jesus and the others, was a Judean (read uppity southerner) may have seemed an unfitting usurpation of James' rightful place, if Judas was at Jesus' left. The request may have been approached as an indirect way of correcting what they saw as a caste faux pas. Surely James would not be denied his appropriate place in the kingdom if the younger John were at the Lord's side.

James could single-handedly keep any spiritual mentor challenged for years. But Jesus had the rest of the apostles, as well as seventy other disciples with which to contend, and a good number of them were just as tempestuous as James. In less than three years, He would have to shape them and propel them all into the church's work of sending and being sent, thus transforming the world.

> James' body may have been taken to northern Spain. His tomb is believed to be at a site rediscovered by a hermit some 800 years later during the Moorish invasion. All of Spain rallied around their newly recognized patron saint against the Moors.
>
> —*Legend*

It is not likely that Jesus called any of His disciples to follow Him because of their existing virtues. Jesus always seemed to have had the vision for all things, of what would be, and, in His view of the disciples, of what they would become. Jesus is the Good Shepherd who calls things that aren't as though they are (Romans 4:17). His followers in all times possess an unmerited dignity imputed to them by His name and fruitful shepherding. The Lord's vision for the twelve was most intimately portrayed in His gathering to Himself of the inner circle.

Larry Hurtado suggests a different perspective on the nickname Jesus gave to James and John. "This kind of suggestion is best taken with a grain of salt," he forewarns. "It is at least as likely that thunder is a symbol of the appearance of the kingdom of God (thunder, earthquakes, etc., are mentioned in the OT in connection with manifestations of God's power). If so, then these two are described simply as supporters or participants in the events of Jesus' ministry . . ."[12] Better still, they are heralds of the kingdom.

The hunger James seems to have had for personal dignity and honor was not satisfied, but was instead reformed into humility and a desire for the Lord's honor and His kingdom. His missionary work may have carried him as far away as Spain, but he was no doubt a servant to believers in Judea, for he brought the wrath of the high priest against him resulting in his execution. A tradition considered reliable and recorded by Clement of Alexandria and others underscores James' new forgiving heart in contrast to the younger, contentious arrogance that wanted to be Elijah (Luke 9:54).

> "In the year 44 Saint James, who was at that time in Jerusalem, was brought before King Herod Agrippa. The Apostle had been preaching fearlessly there, curing the sick and the blind, and delivering possessed persons. Two magicians were sent by the authorities to stop his doings by their charms, but both were converted. His enemies were not defeated by that, however, and paid two Roman captains to incite a sedition during the Apostle's preaching, then seize him as its author. A certain Josias, a scribe among the Pharisees, put a cord around his neck and took him before the third Herod, grandson of the first, murderer of the Innocents, and nephew of the second, who had the Baptist decapitated. This new sycophant of the Roman Emperors, desiring to conciliate the Jews and make them forget his non-Jewish origins, decided to do so by persecuting the Christians. Without delay he

> condemned Saint James to die by the sword. The Apostle's fearless confession of Jesus crucified so moved the scribe Josias, that he too confessed Christ and begged pardon of the Saint. He was taken with the Apostle to the place of execution, where Saint James and his convert died together."

The dialogue between life and providence is echoed in the progress of the apostles' lives. It is seen in the fact that James' thunder was heard more briefly, and most likely by fewer people, outside of Israel than that of any other apostle. The brevity of James' ministry should not be seen exclusively as a consequence of his presumptions. His equally presumptuous brother, John, was chosen, by contrast, to outlive all the other apostles including Paul, to author more books of the New Testament than anyone except Paul, to probably avoid martyrdom to an old age and natural death, and to be highly honored with the responsibility of caring for the Lord's mother. The Lord cut short the service of His faithful servant, James, and was gracious to the life of the second son, John.

First, to the honor-seeking sons of thunder, and also to the whole egocentric world, the Father lovingly speaks into the honored names and lives of the apostles. Although we do honor ourselves to the degree of our willingness to sacrifice all for the kingdom of Christ, it is not hire and salary. All honor and glory belong to the Father who honors whom He wills. And if He wills that a newcomer to the wheat field be counted equal to us who have labored the length and heat of the day, what is that to us? Even our labor and our thunder are His.

Apostolic Symbols and Patronages of James of Zebedee

James is represented in art as a dark-bearded man holding a book, scroll, staff, or sword. He is also occasionally symbolized by one of these items. He may also be seen wearing a pilgrim's hat or on horseback.

James' patronage includes:

- Ω Arthritis sufferers
- Ω Apothecaries and pharmacists
- Ω Blacksmiths, tanners, and laborers
- Ω Equestrians and Spanish conquistadors
- Ω Knights and soldiers
- Ω Pilgrims
- Ω Veterinarians
- Ω The nations of Chile, Guatemala, Nicaragua, and Spain

Memorial

25 July (Western church)

Where to Find James in the Bible[9]

Ω Matthew 4:21	Son of Zebedee
Ω Matthew 4:21	Fisherman
Ω Matthew 10:2	One of the twelve
Ω Luke 5:10	In business with Peter
Ω Mark 3:17	Called Boanerges
Ω Luke 9:52–55	Of fiery disposition
Ω Mark 10:35–45	Makes a contention
Ω Matthew 17:1	One of inner circle
Ω John 21:1, 2	Sees the risen Lord
Ω Acts 1:13	Awaits the Holy Spirit
Ω Acts 12:2	Slain by Herod Agrippa

Chapter Four
John of Zebedee

When Jesus had said these things, He was troubled in spirit, and testified and said, "Most assuredly, I say to you, one of you will betray Me." Then the disciples looked at one another, perplexed about whom He spoke. Now there was leaning on Jesus' bosom one of His disciples, whom Jesus loved. Simon Peter therefore motioned to him to ask who it was of whom He spoke. Then, leaning back on Jesus' breast, he said to Him, "Lord, who is it?" Jesus answered, "It is he to whom I shall give a piece of bread when I have dipped it." And having dipped the bread, He gave it to Judas Iscariot, the son of Simon.

John 13:21–26

With the passing of time, John has become more prominent than his brother, James. It was not so in their own time. Both were fishermen, both were among the first disciples, both are listed among the twelve, and both belong to the inner circle. Their names are mentioned a fairly equal number of times in the synoptic Gospels, and usually they are mentioned together. Even so, John is identified as the disciple Jesus loved in the Fourth Gospel. Then, too, he lived a long and full life and left us a rich literary legacy related to his apostolic mission. The trail should not be difficult to follow.

One day as Jesus was standing by the Sea of Galilee, with a large crowd surrounding him, he saw at the water's edge two boats. He got into one of them, which belonged to Peter, asking to preach to the crowd a short distance from shore. After preaching he said to Peter "Launch out into the deep and let down your nets for a catch" (Luke 5:4). Peter bemoaned the fact that they had worked hard all night without success. But the Lord's preaching had already softened the crusty fisherman's resolve, and he reluctantly yielded to Jesus' bidding. A miraculous abundance of fish so filled the nets that they threatened to break. With excited panic they called out to their partners, James and John, to help them.

All of them were shaken to the core by this event. In all their years of fishing, they had never witnessed anything like it. The Sea of Galilee may as well have parted to accommodate the astonishment of those labor-toughened fishermen. But what they quickly began to see in the Lord's command of such abundance was a messianic sign, because all Hebrews knew that the messianic age was to be a time of plenty. We can also see this great gathering of fish anticipating the great ingathering of the redeemed with the calling voice of the Gospel.

Chapter Four

In probably an hour's time, Jesus had conquered the independent objectives of four self-interested, weather-beaten fishermen, and had brought them into the fellowship of the Shaliach. They immediately left all to be made fishers of men. Little did John and the others know the catch that awaited them.

Early historians agree reliably that John's missionary struggle remained in Asia Minor throughout his life while working out of a base in Ephesus. That the Lord's mother lived the last of her life with John in Ephesus is accepted as fact by Turkish authorities.

—*Legend*

John later recorded from memory how the resurrected Lord performed this first miracle for them again as His last act with them. It happened during His third resurrected appearance to John and others this way: Peter, Thomas, Nathanael, the sons of Zebedee, and two other disciples were together. "I am going fishing," Peter announced. "We are going with you also," they replied (John 21:3). So they went out and fished all night, but caught nothing. Early the next morning Jesus stood on the shore, but they did not recognize Him.

He urged them to cast their net on the right side of the boat. When they did so, they were unable to haul in the net because of the enormous amount of fish! Then the disciple Jesus loved said to Peter, "It is the Lord!" (21:7). When this miracle occurred, the beloved disciple recognized that the Man on the shore was their risen Lord. One can imagine the astonishment and joy in John's voice. The shouting chaos that must have ensued included Peter scrambling to get dressed, but then impatiently jumping into the water, presumably to swim ashore. Imagine that. People usually get undressed when they go for a swim. Peter may have covered himself out of respect for Jesus, but a water-soaked cloak would be dangerously heavy swimwear. This scene must have been humorous and endearing to Jesus. He surely rejoiced at proving Himself faithful to His promise to the apostles that their sorrow would be turned to joy (John 16:19–24). The irrepressible delight they all must have felt is the stuff of which tear-saturated reunions are made. John, as usual, appeared as the more reflective, and Peter, predictably, as more impulsive. But the obvious love they all had for Jesus, punctuated by John's declaration, made their remaining individuality shine for Him.

The disciple Jesus loved is a provocative designation. It takes the place of a personal pronoun that occurs only in John's Gospel when he refers to himself. It seems unlikely that Jesus identified him as such. John likely used this phrase as a personal tribute to his experience of the wonder and magnitude of the love Jesus gave to them all. The eminent theologian Karl Barth was asked, "What is the most profound theological statement ever expressed?" He replied, "Jesus loves me, this I know, for the Bible tells me so." John would have heartily agreed. Truly, all the profundities of men and angels are noise apart from this unsearchable truth. And this same love unconditionally poured out upon John and his brothers is bequeathed to us by them. Their prayer for us is that same plea to the Father Jesus made for them which John alone recorded.

> "As You sent Me into the world, I also have sent them into the world. And for their sakes I sanctify Myself, that they also may be sanctified by the truth. I do not pray for these alone, but also for those who will believe in Me through their word; that they all may be one, as You, Father, are in Me, and I in You; that they also may be one in Us, that the world may believe that You sent Me. And the glory which You gave Me

I have given them, that they may be one just as We are one: I in them, and You in Me; that they may be made perfect in one, and that the world may know that You have sent Me, and have loved them as You have loved Me" (John 17:18–23).

Not to depart in the least from the affection within John's pseudonym, it is also recognizable as a designation of honor, which we previously considered regarding the presumed implications of John's nearness to Jesus upon the kingdom status of both of Salome's boys.

St. Iranaeus states that John wrote his Gospel in Ephesus.
—*Legend*

Following Jesus' laboring intercession for the apostles and all His followers who would come after, the scene shifts to Calvary. Near Jesus' Cross stood His mother, His mother's sister, Mary the wife of Clopas, and Mary Magdalene. When Jesus saw His mother there, and the disciple whom He loved standing nearby, He said to her: "Woman, behold your son!" and to the disciple, "Behold your mother!" (John 19:26–27). From that time on, the disciple took her into his home.

John witnessed and marveled at the dance between suffering and love nailed to a cross as Jesus concerned Himself with the care and forgiveness of others. As a faithful son He enjoined His mother to the care of the one nearest to her, which John gladly welcomed. This may inform us of why Jesus so preferred him generally.

Jesus forgave the Romans and entreated the Father's forgiveness because of their ignorance. How this bodes for the Pharisees He often rebuked and others in all times who are not ignorant and yet have despised and rejected him involves a sobering debate. He promised the penitent thief that he would be with Him in paradise without addressing the scornful thief.

John of Zebedee

Early on the first day of the week, just before dawn, Mary Magdalene went to the tomb where Jesus' body was laid. The stone guarding the tomb was rolled away from its entrance. So she came running to tell Peter and the one Jesus loved, "They have taken away the Lord out of the tomb, and we do not know where they have laid Him" (John 20:2). It seemed the thing to do. Whatever was involved, she trusted that the inner circle could be expected to take decisive action. All they could do, though, was go see with their own eyes. John ran the entire way and made it to the opened tomb before Peter, but he didn't enter. Peter, peering in, saw the evidence of what had happened. There in the niche of the rock were the vacant, hastily applied, preparations of spices and burial cloth—intact. Mary Magdalene and the traveling pair, Cleopas and Simon, reported to the apostles that they had seen the Lord, but they didn't let themselves believe (Mark 16:9–13; Luke 24:13–35) until He showed Himself to them as well. Jesus rebuked their unbelief but mercifully opened their understanding (Luke 24:25–27).

> Eusebius believed that John's banishment to Patmos occurred during the reign of Domitian.
>
> —*Legend*

Jesus appeared to John four times in all, unless two appearances to the apostles spoken of by Paul in 1 Corinthians 15:5, 7 involve occurrences not recorded in the Gospels. On the third occasion, at the Sea of Tiberius (John 21:1) referred to earlier, Jesus took Peter aside to give him one last moment of personal discipling and a word about his martyrdom. "Most assuredly, I say to you," Jesus solemnly told Peter, "when you were younger, you girded yourself and walked where you wished; but when you are old, you will stretch out your hands, and another will gird you and carry you where you do not wish" (John 21:18). "This He spoke, signifying by what death he would glorify God," John adds. Then Jesus enjoined him, "Follow me!" (21:19).

Domitian is said to have had John brought to Rome to answer for alleged threats against Rome. John testified that after Domitians' rule and many others, the King of heaven and earth would rule forever. He backed up his authority by fasting the entire trip to Rome and drinking poison unharmed in front of the Emperor. He then healed a sick relative of Domitians. John was not released but was sent to the penal colony on Patmos. After his release, he lived again in Ephesus until his death about A.D. 100.

—*Legend*

Peter turned and observed that the disciple Jesus loved was following them. "But Lord," he inquired of Jesus, "what about this man?" Jesus answered, "If I will that he remain till I come, what is that to you? You follow Me" (John 21:22). This gave rise to the rumor that this disciple would not die. However, John assures us that this was not Jesus' intent. He merely reminded Peter that this was not his concern.

Peter may have raised this question out of mere curiosity. One can imagine, though, that what Jesus revealed about Peter's end distressed him enough to momentarily question the Lord's apparent favoritism of John. John uncovers the wisdom of this lesson to all believers beginning with Peter about single-minded devotion. We cannot buy our redemption, which was already paid for with Christ's all. He has no need to purchase from us our trust in Him and commitment to follow Him with any promise of lives that compare well with each other or otherwise compensate our suffering.

Papius, the early third century bishop of Hieropolis, knew a disciple of Johns' also named John and called "the Elder" who told Papius that the apostle John was indeed martyred by the Jews fulfilling, along with James, that which Jesus foretold would be their shared cup with Him. Origen agrees about the martyrdom of John in his commentary of Matthew.

—*Legend*

Nevertheless, John's advanced age when he probably wrote these words may account for the development of the axiom about him leaving this life naturally. Whether this report is accurate or whether he died a natural death, what is revealing in the above quoted passage about the young disciple Jesus loved, is that John was not content to be separated from the Lord again for even a moment so he followed behind them (John 21:20). Even as a young disciple not yet empowered by the Holy Spirit, the evidence of his years with Jesus was strong. John had become a man whom Jesus could trust to love His mother as He would. He alone showed no fear, though he must have felt some, of the Romans or Jesus' enemies at Golgotha. He was the first to recognize the Lord at the Sea of Tiberius. It was he who made the preparations for the Last

Supper, so he not only served Jesus but the others as well. He was overwhelmed his entire life with Jesus; marveling in his old age that the world could not contain books enough to catalog His wonders (John 21:25). John didn't just love and serve the Lord Jesus. He yearned for Him.

The Name of John

John is an English rendering of the Greek translation of John's name. In Hebrew, John would have been called Yochanan which means "Yahweh is gracious." Little needs to be said to uncover the provident fulfillment of that phrase for John, the son of Zebedee. The grace of just knowing Jesus face to face is beyond the comprehension of the multitude of us who have never seen or heard Him in the flesh. We have no idea what He looked or sounded like. John was the disciple who Jesus most loved who leaned on Jesus' bosom. He cared for Mary until her own death. He wrote Scripture and led the Lord's worldwide church until an old age. And even when he drank the cup of sorrows and suffered at times, he loved well and enjoined us all to love one another. God was gracious to John, the apostle of love, and to us through him.

Apostolic Symbols and Patronages of John of Zebedee

John is represented by an eagle symbolizing him as an evangelist; a cup and a serpent, alluding to the Lords' cup of sorrows he was to drink; a cauldron, alluding to the martyrdom of his will though not in death; and a book or a chalice.

John's patronage includes:

- Ω Theologians
- Ω Writers, editors, publishers, bookbinders, and booksellers
- Ω Engravers, painters, printers, and typesetters

- Ω Art dealers
- Ω Tanners
- Ω Poisoning
- Ω Cleveland, Ohio, Taos, New Mexico, and Asia Minor

Memorials

27 December (Western church)
8 May (Eastern church)

Where to Find John in the Bible[9]

Life of:

Ω Matthew 4:21	Son of Zebedee
Ω Luke 5:1–11	Fisherman
Ω Matthew 4:21, 22	Leaves his business for Christ
Ω Matthew 10:2	Called to be an apostle
Ω Mark 13:3, Luke 9:54, 55	Rebuked by Christ
Ω Luke 22:8–13	Sent to prepare Passover
Ω John 13:23–25	Close to Jesus at Last Supper
Ω John 19:26, 27	Christ commits His mother to
Ω Acts 1:9–13	Witnesses Christ's Ascension
Ω Acts 3:1–11	With Peter, heals a man
Ω Acts 4:1–21	Imprisoned with Peter
Ω Acts 8:14–25	With Peter, becomes a missionary
Ω Galatians 2:9	Encourages Paul
Ω Revelation 1:9	Exiled on Patmos
Ω John 21:23–25	Wrote a Gospel
Ω 1 John, 2 John, 3 John	Wrote three epistles
Ω Revelation 1:1, 4, 9	Wrote the Revelation

Chapter Four

Described as:

Ω Acts 4:13	Uneducated
Ω Mark 9:38	Intolerant
Ω Mark 10:35–37	Ambitious
Ω John 19:26, 27	Trustworthy
Ω Revelation 19:10	Humble
Ω John 21:20	Beloved by Jesus

Chapter Five
Andrew

John stood with two of his disciples. And looking at Jesus . . . he said, "Behold! The Lamb of God!" The two disciples heard him speak, and they followed Jesus. One of the two who . . . followed Him, was Andrew, Simon Peter's brother. He first found his own brother Simon, and said to him, "We have found the Messiah."

John 1:35–41

Finding Jesus established a course for Andrew to spend the rest of his life seeking and finding people who would be instrumental in spreading the gospel. He was known as the "Protocletus" (the First Called), as he was the first apostle chosen by Jesus. But he receives little individual notice throughout the Bible beyond that distinction.

He was content with lesser fame as a humble and unassuming man, and yet his single-minded devotion to Christ was unfaltering. It gave him an inner strength that propelled him to fulfill the meaning of his name—strong man; conqueror—and to carry on the Shaliach tradition of preparing students to become teachers of the Word.

> During one of Andrew's ministry treks to Patras, Greece, sometime between A.D. 60 and 69, Governor Aegeates ordered his execution by crucifixion on a transverse cross, which resembles a capital X.
>
> —*Legend*

Andrew was the son of Joanna and a fisherman named John. He had one brother, Simon, who Jesus renamed Peter. Andrew originally came from Bethsaida and later lived in Capernaum. It was in Capernaum that Andrew owned fishing craft and the means to carry on a profitable business. He was in partnership with his brother, and the brothers of Zebedee, James and John (Luke 5:7, 10).

Despite his successful business venture, which is every man's dream, Andrew must have felt an overwhelming call to some loftier service because he initially dropped his nets to follow John the Baptist. He heard John preach about the coming of Jesus, and watched as the people came to him to be baptized. Soon, he was assisting John the Baptist and preparing for the day the Messiah would come.

It is not known, exactly, where Andrew's body was laid to rest, but around 357, Emperor Constantine had Andrew's body moved to the Church of the Holy Apostles in Constantinople. According to Mary Sharp's *A Traveler's Guide to Saints in Europe*, Pope Pius II transferred Andrew's head to St. Peter's in Rome in 1462. In 1964, Pope Paul VI gave St. Andrew's head to the Greek Orthodox Church in Patras. Some of Andrew's remains may have also been interred in Russia.[13]

—*Legend*

When that day arrived, Andrew was present as Jesus of Nazareth emerged from the crowd to be baptized by John. "Behold! The Lamb of God who takes away the sin of the world!" John exclaimed. "This is He of whom I said, 'After me comes a Man who is preferred before me, for He was before me'" (John 1:29–30). Andrew knew that this was true without doubt, so he immediately left John and became a faithful follower of Jesus. Soon afterward, he brought his brother, Peter, to Jesus, as well as his business partners, James and John, and later, his friend, Philip.

Andrew's association with his brother, Peter, seemed to thrust him into prominence from time to time, but his link to John the Baptist should be viewed as more significant, for it documents the transition of focus from John to Jesus. As a disciple of John the Baptist, Andrew was given to enlisting other disciples, so it was inevitable that his brother, Peter, would be brought to Jesus (John 1:35–42). Andrew's dedication to ministry paid rich dividends through the people he brought to Christ—namely his brother, Peter.

> Andrew raised 39 sailors from the dead after they washed ashore following a shipwreck.
>
> —*Legend*

Following his first unforgettable encounter with Jesus, Andrew returned to Capernaum and his fishing endeavors. He must have been very excited about sharing his experience with his family and friends. But then, Jesus found him again, working alongside his brother, and He extended the invitation to make them "fishers of men." Unable and apparently unwilling to resist, Andrew and Peter knew what they must do. They literally dropped everything to follow Him (Matthew 4:18–20).

> Andrew endured imprisonment, stoning, and even the threat of being eaten by cannibals.
>
> —*Legend*

To be chosen as the first apostle must have been an astounding honor, but Andrew could not have known what it would be like when he traveled with Peter, Philip, and John with Jesus to a wedding at Cana. He was present as Jesus performed His first miracle—turning water into wine (John 2:1–11).

Simon Peter accepted his invitation to be "fishers of men" in a more gregarious manner, preferring to draw large groups of converts. But Andrew, in the early days of his discipleship, held his task in equal esteem by bringing believers to faith one at a time. However, the ones he brought were very big fish, indeed.

Andrew sought to rescue the apostle Matthias from pirates and cannibals on an island in the Black Sea, but was captured and nearly killed. He cured fellow prisoners of blindness and so moved his captors by his eloquent gospel, that he and Matthias were released and the entire population of the island was converted.

—Legend

His particular style of witnessing developed like a single raindrop falling on a clear, still pond. His deeply personal approach consisted of converting those closest to him first—his brother, other family members; then his business associates and closest friends. Like the ripples caused by the raindrop, Andrew's ministry reached far from the hub of his existence, gaining momentum as it spread. He traveled across thousands of miles of land and ocean to spread the Word.

Andrew's focused recruiting ability was recorded many times in the Bible. In one instance, Jesus went up on a mountainside and sat down with His disciples. He looked up and saw a great crowd coming toward Him. He inquired of Philip, "Where shall we buy bread that these may eat?" (John 6:5). Philip answered, "Two hundred denarii worth of bread is not sufficient for them, that every one of them may have a little." At this, Andrew volunteered, "There is a lad here who has five barley loaves and two small fish, but what are they among so many?" (6:7–9). How did Andrew come upon this boy? Richard Bauman, in *Story, Performance, and Event,* speculates that "his knowledge of the lad came as a result of a reconnaissance with a view to finding out what food resources could be mustered . . . Or the boy may have offered his food to Jesus."[14] In any case, Andrew runs true to form by bringing another crucial character to the attention of Jesus and into the intriguing plot of His message.

In Patras, Achaia, a magistrate on Andrew's trial demanded, "Are you Andrew, who destroys the temples of the gods, and persuades men about the religion which, having lately made its appearance, the emperors of the Romans have given orders to suppress?" A dazzling light engulfed Andrew, and remained for a half hour. "And when he had thus spoken and glorified the Lord still more, the light withdrew itself, and he gave up the ghost, and along with the brightness itself he departed to the Lord in giving Him thanks."

—*Legend*

That characteristic response of finding people is seen again in John 12:21. Some Greeks went to Jerusalem for the festival and made a request of Philip. "Sir," they said, "we wish to see Jesus." Philip went to tell Andrew, and they went together to tell Jesus. Perhaps Philip wasn't sure what to do. But the Greeks seemed to represent the Gentile world, and Andrew was familiar with his commission to share with them the Good News of salvation to all people.

After Andrew was officially named a disciple of Jesus, he spent the next two and one-half years learning from Him and was witness to many more history-shaping events. As mentioned before, he was present at the feeding of the masses at the Sea of Galilee, but he was also present at the Feast of the Passover (Matthew 26:20), and the Sermon on the Mount (5:1).

Governor Aegeates, of Patras Greece, was apparently angry that his wife, Maximilla, converted to Christianity when she heard Andrew's passionate preaching. To make matters worse for the unrepentant governor, his brother, Stratoklis, was also converted and Andrew ordained him as the first bishop of Patras. The governor, who was furious about the conversions taking place in his own household and his inability to change their minds, had Andrew crucified on a transverse cross.

—*Legend*

Following the Ascension, Andrew began his ministry in Scythia, Russia. He also founded parishes in Asia Minor, Thrace, Macedonia, Vithynia and Pontus, Greece, and eventually Byzantium (Constantinople). He holds the honor of being the Patron Saint of Scotland, as well.

The Name of Andrew

The biblical name Andrew means "strong, manly, and conqueror." To be the first called as a disciple of John the Baptist, and then to Jesus, Andrew must have exhibited great strength of character to withstand the negative aspects faced by all trailblazers throughout history. Andrew must have felt a fair amount of fear and trepidation in those early days, what with naysayers, heretics and false prophets, and Christian persecutors in his midst.

> Andrew boldly proclaimed his faith to thousands during his execution and encouraged all to be faithful to Christ.
>
> —*Legend*

Upon leaving a lucrative fishing business and traveling from town to town with Jesus, he must have felt at least a little uncertainty about his future. But, great leaders of the world are not born as leaders. They follow first, learning from their mentors, and spending many years making mistakes and asking questions before taking over the reigns.

> The public was outraged at Andrew's pending death. At one point, the Consul ordered him to be released. But Andrew would not have it. He insisted that he would not be taken down while he was alive.
>
> —*Legend*

His greatest sorrow must have been witnessing the death of his mentor and savior, Jesus Christ. On the other hand, his greatest joy must have been seeing Christ again following the Resurrection, and knowing that his mission was set in stone. Andrew must have felt certain that, upon his own death, he would be with his Lord again, and that eternal truth kept him going in the face of adversity.

Governor Aegeates beseeched Andrew to denounce his faith in order to save his own life. Conversely, Andrew urged Aegeates to save his soul by turning to Christ.

—*Legend*

Andrew's strength was evident and growing from the beginning of his discipleship with John the Baptist, and continued growing while bringing people, one by one, and then by the thousands, to Jesus Christ. He conquered many lands and many hearts, founded churches, and charmed the hardest adversaries with his eloquent ministry.

Governor Aegeates wife, Maximilla, and his brother, Bishop Stratoklis, took Andrew's body from the cross and buried it.

—*Legend*

If his manner of death is fact, rather than legend, then it was the last symbol of fulfillment for his namesake. Even while he was dying, he proclaimed his faith in Christ. He converted thousands even while his hands were bound. He was bathed in the Holy Spirit during his last breaths and committed his soul to life everlasting with a joyful heart. The man who would be Andrew, the First Called, was a strong man of faith and a conqueror of darkness to the very end of his life.

Chapter Five

Apostolic Symbols and Patronages of Andrew

Andrew is symbolized by an old man leaning on a transverse cross, with the gospel in his right hand. This transverse cross is now known as "St. Andrew's Cross."

Andrew's patronage is linked to:

- Achaia and Patras, Greece
- Amalfi, Italy
- Scotland
- Diocese of Constantinople
- University of Patras in Greece
- Fishermen and anglers
- Maidens and unmarried women
- Old maids and spinsters
- Women who want children
- Singers and sore throats
- Gout

Memorial

30 November

Where to Find Andrew in the Bible[9]

Matthew 4:18	A fisherman
John 1:40	A disciple of John the Baptist
John 1:40–42	Brought Peter to Christ
Matthew 4:18, 19	Called to Christ's discipleship
Matthew 10:2	Enrolled among the twelve
John 6:8, 9	Told Jesus about a lad's lunch
John 12:20–22	Carried a request to Jesus

Andrew

Ω Mark 13:3, 4	Sought further light on Jesus' words
Ω Acts 1:13	Met in the Upper Room

Other brief mentions

- Ω Mark, 1:16, 1:29, 3:18
- Ω Luke 6:14

Chapter Six
Philip

Jesus said to him, "I am the way, the truth, and the life. No one comes to the Father except through Me. If you had known Me, you would have known My Father also; and from now on you know Him and have seen Him." Philip said to Him, "Lord, show us the Father, and it is sufficient for us." Jesus said to him, "Have I been with you so long, and yet you have not known Me, Philip? He who has seen Me has seen the Father; so how can you say, 'Show us the Father'? Do you not believe that I am in the Father, and the Father in Me? The words that I speak to you I do not speak on My own authority; but the Father who dwells in Me does the works. Believe Me that I am in the Father and the Father in Me, or else believe Me for the sake of the works themselves."

John 14:6–11

This passage highlights the inquisitive nature of one of the most passionate and evangelistic of the twelve apostles: Philip. A thoughtful, caring man who had a talent for asking the hard questions, Philip, like the apostle Andrew, also had a gift for bringing people to Jesus Christ. Although he was called third (following Peter and Andrew), he was the first to bring another person to meet the Man to whom he would dedicate his faith and his life.

Philip is often described as youthful, naïve, and shy, presumably because there is no mention which assigns to him the proud, willful, brooding, deceitful, or aggressive nature that is apparent in most of the other apostles.

After the Ascension, Philip first preached and worked miracles in Galilee, where he restored life to a dead infant in its mother's arms.

—*Legend*

Although Philip is only mentioned in the list of apostles in the synoptic Gospels (Matthew 10:3; Mark 3:18; Luke 6:14; see also Acts 1:13), John gives us a full portrait of a man devoted to God. It would be easy to assume that Philip was the unidentified one of the two disciples of John the Baptist who followed Jesus, because Andrew, who was from Philip's hometown of Bethsaida, was named as the other. This is supported by the fact that when certain Greeks came to Philip seeking Jesus, he first reported to Andrew who joined him in presenting the visitors (John 12:20–22). It is also noteworthy that both Andrew and Philip immediately testified that Jesus was the Messiah, no doubt following preparation by John the Baptist (John

1:41, 45). No other such testimony is spoken by any of the twelve until Simon Peter about three years later.

Born in Bethsaida, a village in Galilee, Philip responded without hesitation when Jesus said to him, "Follow Me" (John 1:43–44). Some scholars believe that Philip must have been well schooled in the Law and the prophets to not only recognize Jesus as the Messiah, but to desire to share this news right away.

Philip traveled extensively in Greece, baptizing many and appointing Herod's bishop in Hieropolis.

—Legend

Jesus called him the day after He chose Peter and Andrew, and immediately, Philip found someone else to bring to Jesus. In the Gospels of Matthew, Mark, and Luke, Philip is paired with Bartholomew (Matthew 10:3; Mark 3:18; Luke 6:14; see also Acts 1:13). In the Gospel of John, however, there is no mention of Bartholomew, but Nathanael is found by Philip and brought to Jesus (John 1:45). When Nathanael expressed his doubt about Jesus' Messiahship, Philip echoed a phrase from Jesus when he said, "Come and see" (John 1:39, 46). Philip was so sure in his belief, he knew Nathanael would meet Jesus and see His ministry and he would believe, too.

Philip certainly saw enough evidence that he was convinced without ado. Only three days after joining Jesus on His journey, he, along with the other apostles, witnessed the first miracle at the wedding at Cana (2:1–11). From the beginning, Philip was privy to the power and glory of Christ. Many of these miracles happened in Philip's own hometown of Bethsaida, including the healing of a blind man (Mark 8:22).

Philip

The feeding of the multitude took place not far from Bethsaida (see Mark 6:45), which may be the reason Jesus turned to Philip regarding food for the massive crowd. Jesus saw this as the perfect time to test Philip's faith in Him as the Son of God, when He asked, "Where shall we buy bread, that these may eat?" (John 6:5). The exchange between Jesus and Philip here regarding the purchase of bread is curious. Jesus knew what was about to happen, and Philip, sensible and practical, knew the strength of Jesus' power and compassion. He had already witnessed His miracles. Philip responded that it would take more than a year's wage to give each even a bite of food. Sometimes, reason has to be set aside in the face of great faith, as Jesus demonstrated when He performed an impossible task: feeding a great crowd on five loaves of bread and two fish (6:5–11). Philip had a front-row seat to the proof that nothing is impossible for the Son of God.

> One particular legend, the "Golden Legend," claims that Philip drove away a dragon at the Temple of Mars using a cross.
>
> —*Legend*

Yet Philip's search for proof didn't end there. He was still hungry to be "shown," even as the apostles celebrated the Passover in the Upper Room. When Jesus spoke of the Father, Philip asked, impatiently, "Lord, show us the Father, and it is sufficient for us." Jesus, however, used Philip's need to send the message of His divinity to the world. "Have I been with you so long, and yet you have not known Me, Philip? He who has seen Me has seen the Father" (John 14:9). Since the primary theme of John's Gospel is the divinity of Jesus Christ, Philip provides an intelligent and sound pivotal point for that message.

Snake cult pagans crucified Philip with Bartholomew in Phrygian Hieropolis, but the prayers of Philip for the redemption of the pagans, plus a sudden earthquake, frightened them into expediting the apostles' release. Bartholomew survived, but Philip had already died. Philip's sister, Marianna, who had been traveling with him, buried him there in Hieropolis and then traveled with Bartholomew to Armenia after baptizing many of the pagans.

—*Legend*

Philip's need for proof may echo a similar desire in believers today, but Philip's questioning of Jesus did not represent doubts. Philip's faith in Jesus as the Messiah was so well known, that when a group of Greeks (possibly Hellenistic Jews) wanted to meet and hear Christ, they went to Philip (John 12:20–22). Perhaps one reason that Jesus tested Philip, and addressed him directly, was that He knew that Philip was asking the right questions—the questions that would be put to believers throughout all time.

Following Philip's request to Jesus in the Upper Room, he is only mentioned one other time in the New Testament (he should not be confused with the deacon whose ministry is discussed later in Acts). Following Christ's Ascension, Philip was present with the rest of the disciples when the Holy Spirit anointed each of them.

Tradition, however, holds that Philip lived to an old age, teaching and preaching the Word of God, possibly in Phrygia (Turkey), where angry pagans murdered him. In A.D. 194, Bishop Polycrates of Antioch wrote, "Philip, one of the twelve apostles, sleeps at Hieropolis."

> The church historian, Eusebius, cites Polycrates, Bishop of Ephesus (later 2nd century), who reported that Philip was a family man with three daughters, two of which were buried in Hieropolis, while the third rested in Ephesus.
>
> —*Legend*

While this cannot be verified, there is no doubt that Philip loved Christ, and that he never stopped seeking the face of the Father.

Apostolic Symbols and Patronages of Philip

Philip is represented in art as an elderly man with a beard, holding a basket of bread loaves and a T-shaped cross.

He is the patron saint of Luxembourg and Uruguay.

Memorials

3 May (Western church)
14 November (Eastern church)

Where to Find Philip in the Bible[9]

Ω Matthew 10:3	One of the twelve apostles
Ω John 1:43–48	Brought Nathanael to Christ

Chapter Six

Ω John 6:5–7	Tested by Christ to feed 5,000
Ω John 12:20–22	Introduced Greeks to Christ
Ω John 14:8–12	Gently rebuked by Christ
Ω Acts 1:13	In the Upper Room

Chapter Seven
Bartholomew

And He went up on the mountain and called to Him those He Himself wanted. And they came to Him. Then He appointed twelve, that they might be with Him and that He might send them out to preach, and to have power to heal sicknesses and to cast out demons: Simon, to whom He gave the name Peter; James the son of Zebedee and John the brother of James, to whom He gave the name Boanerges, that is, "Sons of Thunder"; Andrew, Philip, Bartholomew, Matthew, Thomas, James the son of Alphaeus, Thaddaeus, Simon the Cananite; and Judas Iscariot, who also betrayed Him. And they went into a house.

Mark 3:13–19

Bartholomew is one of a small group of apostles who are known merely because of their names in the list of twelve. Almost nothing else is known about him, except for one significant, historical fact: Jesus wanted Bartholomew near Him. That fact alone builds a picture of an ordinary man who had extraordinary faith and love for Christ. He was given exceptional spiritual gifts and sent out to proclaim the message of God throughout the world.

> Bartholomew preached in a part of remote Arabia then known as part of India. He also preached in Armenia. It was in Abanopolis in western Armenia near the Caspian Sea where Bartholomew is said to have been flayed (skinned) alive and then beheaded.
>
> —*Legend*

Bartholomew's name, which means "son of Talmai," (or Tholmai) could be his patronymic name, although Scripture does not specifically mention his father. "Talmai," however, was an ancient Hebrew name (one of David's fathers-in-law was Talmai, King of Geshur, 2 Samuel 3:3), which provides the only clue to Bartholomew's heritage. There is some speculation that he is the same as the apostle, Nathanael because, while Bartholomew appears in the other four lists of the apostles in the Bible (Matthew 10:3; Mark 3:18; Luke 6:14; Acts 1:13), John never mentions him. Conversely, Nathanael, who appears in John (John 1:45–49), does not appear in the other gospels.

In addition, in the synoptic lists, Bartholomew is always paired with Philip, whereas John mentions that Philip brought Nathanael to Jesus. There is no assurance in Scripture, however, that Bartholomew and Nathanael are the same person, and they are usually treated as two separate individuals.

His relics are said to have been interred on the island of Lipara and eventually transferred to Benevento, Italy, then Rome, where the church of Saint Bartholomew on Isola San Bartolomeo in the Tiber claims them. One of his arms was reportedly given to Canterbury in the 11th century by King Canute's wife, Queen Emma (Benedictines, Bentley, Delaney, Farmer). Relics of Bartholomew are claimed by a church named for him in Rome where they were removed to, from their original resting place on the island of Lipara near Sicily.

—*Legend*

Because there is no other mention of Bartholomew in Scripture, nothing of his life away from the presence of Christ is known with certainty. The listing of Bartholomew alongside Philip may have meant that these two preached together when Jesus sent out His apostles two-by-two to spread the gospel message. Eusebius later wrote that a copy of the Hebrew text of the Gospel of Matthew was found in India, supposedly left there by Bartholomew. "India" could mean Ethiopia, since Eusebius used "India" to indicate a variety of countries. However, the Syriac tradition, which dates at least a century prior to Eusebius, clearly associates Thomas with (East

Asia) India. This is confirmed by later sources as well (see, for instance, Samuel Moffett's *A History of Christianity in Asia*). Church tradition also says that Bartholomew preached in Armenia and Ethiopia, and that King Astyages of Babylon ordered him flayed and beheaded because Bartholomew had converted his brother, King Polymius, and the citizens of twelve cities to Christianity.

In Sao Pedro Do Sul, Portugal, mothers threaten their disobedient children with the "screw of Saint Bartholomew." This may be an instrument of torture and Portuguese children are afraid of Saint Bartholomew.

—*Legend*

While all of this would indicate a remarkable ministry from a gifted teacher and preacher, most of it is conjecture. What is known is that when Jesus called Bartholomew to be an apostle, He changed the life and path of one man, who, in turn, helped change the world.

An apocryphal gospel of Bartholomew existed in the early ages.

—*Legend*

Apostolic Symbols and Patronages of Bartholomew

The apostolic symbol most associated with Bartholomew is a tanner's knife. Sometimes, he is depicted as an elderly man holding a tanner's knife and a human skin. In Portuguese tradition, he is depicted similarly to the Greek god, Poseidon, holding a trident or sword in his hand, with a creature at his feet that looks like a small dog or a fish.

Eusebius reported that Pantenus of Alexandra found a Gospel of Saint Matthew scribed in Hebrew in the northern region of India that was left there by Bartholomew.

—*Legend*

Bartholomew's patronage is linked to:

- Armenia
- Bookbinders
- Butchers, cobblers, and shoemakers
- Florentine cheese and salt merchants
- Leather workers, tanners, and trappers
- Nervous disorders and neurological diseases and twitching

Other traditions report St. Bartholomew preaching in Mesopotamia, Persia, Egypt, Armenia, Lycaonia, Phrygia, and on the shores of the Black Sea.

—*Legend*

In Portugal, he is the patron saint of:

- Sailors and fishermen
- Everyone who lives near rivers or bridges

Memorials

24 August (Western church)
11 June (Eastern church)

Where to Find Bartholomew in the Bible[9]

Ω Acts 1:13	One of Christ's apostles who was in the Upper Room
Ω Matthew 10:3	One of the apostles called by Christ
Ω Mark 3:18	One of the apostles called by Christ
Ω Luke 6:14	One of the apostles called by Christ

Chapter Eight
Matthew

As Jesus passed on from there, He saw a man named Matthew sitting at the tax office. And He said to him, "Follow Me." So he arose and followed Him. Now it happened, as Jesus sat at the table in the house, that behold, many tax collectors and sinners came and sat down with Him and His disciples. And when the Pharisees saw it, they said to His disciples, "Why does your Teacher eat with tax collectors and sinners?" When Jesus heard that, He said to them, "Those who are well have no need of a physician, but those who are sick. But go and learn what this means: 'I desire mercy and not sacrifice.' For I did not come to call the righteous, but sinners, to repentance."

Matthew 9:9–13

When Jesus called His apostles, He chose, for the most part, quite ordinary men. Some were fishermen, some had families, while others were carpenters. They were not prominent officials, nor did they have much of a public life. Matthew, however, made his living while working with the public—and he was despised for it. Calling Matthew as a disciple was quite a strategic and dangerous move, for Jesus was bringing into His inner circle precisely the type of person He was trying to reach most—a sinner.

Matthew, who is also called Levi (Mark 2:14; Luke 5:27–28), was likely a customs official, collecting duty taxes on goods passing through Capernaum. Tax collectors were a dreadfully hated lot. Most of them had advance agreements with the authorities about how much money they would pay for the right to collect taxes, and they were allowed to keep any excess over and above what they collected.

Rampant corruption was a way of life, but it would not only ensure a good income, but also criticism for collaborating with an oppressive political system. Because of their greed and willingness to work with the Romans, Jewish tax collectors were considered unclean and sinful. Righteous people shunned them as a matter of course.

Jesus, however, approached Matthew as he sat at his tax collector's booth. "Follow me," Jesus said, and Matthew rose to his feet and followed Him—just like that (Matthew 9:9). Matthew's response was obedient, decisive, and sacrificial. It was obedient because he did as directed. It was decisive because he did not linger. And it was sacrificial because he left everything (Luke 5:28).

While Jesus was having dinner at Matthew's house later, they were joined by many other tax collectors and sinners. They probably couldn't believe that a man with Jesus' reputation would lower Himself to have dinner with a tax collector, let alone a gaggle of them. The sinners were common folk who, for reason of vocation or disposition, were not religiously scrupulous.

When the Pharisees witnessed what was going on at the house of Matthew, they inquired of Jesus' disciples: "Why does your Teacher eat with tax collectors and sinners?" (Matthew 9:11).

There are various and sometimes conflicting accounts of missionary travel throughout Greece and Asia, but most agree on Asian Ethiopia, Persia, Macedonia, and Syria.

—*Legend*

Overhearing what they said, Jesus observed: "It is not the healthy who need a doctor, but the sick. But go and learn what this means: 'I desire mercy, not sacrifice' (see Hosea 6:6). For I have not come to call the righteous, but sinners" (9:12–13). In keeping with the prophetic text, Jesus does not reject religious ritual, but considers it less important than one's relationship to God and care for others.

Matthew is subsequently listed among the apostles (Matthew 10:3; Mark 3:18; Luke 6:15) and among those awaiting the Coming of the Holy Spirit (Acts 1:13). Other than these instances, no more is said concerning him. It is as if he fades into the background. Tradition has him preaching to the Hebrews for another fifteen years—and possibly carrying the Gospel into Persia. In any case, his former profession would have primed him for the task of setting forth the Good News, even at the risk of being rejected by the masses.

Whether Matthew is actually the author of the Gospel bearing his name, however, has been the topic of significant debate.

The most promising explanation has been that Matthew, as an eyewitness to the ministry of Jesus Christ, collected much of what is in the Gospel in Aramaic, which Bishop Papias of Hieropolis in A.D. 130 referred to as Matthew's "oracles." The common consensus among scholars today is that a second author expanded on Matthew's work, possibly using Mark as a source, to produce, in Greek, the testimony known today as "The Gospel According to Matthew." The Gospel has always been a favorite of the church, which has long used it to teach unbelievers and bring renewal to the faithful.

> Early historians agree that Mathew first preached among the Hebrews, possibly for as long as fourteen years, during which time he wrote his Gospel in Hebrew.
>
> —*Legend*

The striking thing about Matthew's Gospel is that it is divided into five primary collections of instruction, followed by a variation of "when Jesus had ended these sayings" (Matthew 7:28; 11:1; 13:53; 19:1; 26:1). They deal with, in succession, the new community, the new posturing, the ways of the kingdom, in pursuit of excellence, and the future from the present.

The New Community

Matthew takes the reader, almost immediately, to the scene of Jesus teaching a large gathering of people. Jesus was an acclaimed rabbi (teacher), but He does not seem to have had any specialized training in this regard. People are amazed at His teachings, initially because He teaches as One with authority, and not One who relies on religious precedent. He is no doubt charismatic, in the sense of being able to inspire loyalty and devotion from His followers. It was perhaps the same quality that eventually proved a threat to His opposition, so He is not a person to be taken lightly.

The disciples suffered by comparison. They were slow to learn, and were sometimes impetuous. On other occasions, they dragged their feet. Some even turned back. They were summoned to forsake all, the good and the bad alike. Either might be an impediment to following Jesus. One cannot serve two masters, after all. They would, in response, embrace all, for better and for worse. Whatever the benefits of discipleship, they would reap them. Whatever the cost, they would be called upon to pay it. Ultimately, they were not allowed to negotiate the conditions of discipleship.

The call to discipleship, however, also proved to be a call to community. They found themselves as part of a fellowship distinguished only in its relationship to Jesus. All else was immaterial; all else could be deceiving. With the passing of time, they would increasingly become a cross-section of society.

Then, there was the multitude. It constituted the vast majority. Its disposition was mixed. Some were simply curious, others were opportunistic, and still others were seeking. The disciples had once been part of that multitude. They could recall what it was like to walk in darkness. Now they were called to become the light of the world.

Rabbi, disciples, and multitude—they gathered together on a mountainside overlooking the Sea of Galilee. Jesus' reputation had been instrumental in drawing people to that location, and His words would hold their attention. It was instruction time.

"Blessed are the poor in spirit," Jesus announced, "for theirs is the kingdom of heaven. Blessed are those who mourn, for they shall be comforted. Blessed are the meek, for they shall inherit the earth. Blessed are those who hunger and thirst for righteousness, for they shall be filled" (Matthew 5:3–6). One is blessed in a manner similar to that in Psalm 1:1, and is blessed in the sense of enjoying peace with God and the prospect of an inviting future.

He went on to explain more blessings, then cautioned, "Do not think that I came to destroy the Law or the Prophets. I did not come to destroy but to fulfill" (Matthew 5:17). This does not preclude, however, Jesus' use of the refrain, "You have heard that it was said . . . but I say to you" (see 5:21–22). In other words, Jesus did not contradict what was said. However, Jesus uncovers the root of the problem with the disposition that, given the opportunity, leads to evil behavior. In taking this approach, He laid siege to those who would live the letter, but ignore the spirit, of the teaching.

The early church father, Clement of Alexandria, quotes Heracleon in the claim that Matthew was not martyred. This conflicts with many apocryphal documents, most of which are Gnostic and devoid of historical value. The Roman Martyrology merely states that he was martyred in Ethiopia.

—*Legend*

" 'Take heed that you do not do your charitable deeds before men, to be seen by them,' Jesus admonished (Matthew 6:1). 'But when you do a charitable deed, do not let your left hand know what your right hand is doing, that your charitable deed may be in secret; and your Father who sees in secret will Himself reward you openly' " (6:3–4). Then, should someone express his or her appreciation, it comes as a bonus rather than as a requirement.

" 'And when you pray,' Jesus continues, 'you shall not be like the hypocrites. For they love to pray standing in the synagogues and on the corners of the streets, that they may be seen by men. Assuredly, I say to you, they have their reward. But you, when you pray, go into your room, and when you have shut your door, pray to your Father who is in the secret place; and your Father who sees in secret will reward you openly'" (Matthew 6:5–6).

In these and other ways, Jesus encouraged His disciples to commit their ways to God. His teachings urged His listeners to look to the eternal, not the temporal, to build up treasures in heaven, not on earth. As He goes on to stress, building a house with its foundation "on the rock" (7:25), He is teaching them also about building a new community of faith—the church.

The New Posturing

When Jesus saw the multitudes, "He was moved with compassion for them, because they were weary and scattered, like sheep having no shepherd" (Matthew 9:36). Whereupon He observed to His disciples: "The harvest truly is plentiful, but the laborers are few. Therefore pray the Lord of the harvest to send out laborers into His harvest" (9:37–38). The need is urgent, the task great, and the laborers few. Such would encourage frantic activity, but instead, Jesus enjoins prayer. If not for God, their efforts would be in vain.

After this, Jesus summoned His apostles, and sent them out with the following instructions: "Do not go into the way of the Gentiles, and do not enter a city of the Samaritans. But go rather to the lost sheep of the house of Israel" (10:5–6).

"And as you go," Jesus continues, "preach, saying, 'The kingdom of heaven is at hand.' Heal the sick, cleanse the lepers, raise the dead, cast out demons. Freely you have received, freely give. Provide neither gold nor silver nor copper in your money belts, nor bag for your journey, nor two tunics, nor sandals, nor staffs; for a worker is worthy of his food" (10:7–10).

They were to preach and heal. The two merged together in anticipation of God's righteous rule. They were to travel light and be unencumbered with things. The road was difficult enough without making it more so. They had to assume the mentality of a pilgrim, who allows that the world is not his or her own, and whatever they collected along the way, would eventually be left behind. They were to focus on their mission and not the ways of the world.

The world, however, would not always embrace them. Jesus continues to offer cautions and encouragement about what lay before them through the end of chapter 10.

"Therefore whoever confesses Me before men," Jesus allows, "him I will also confess before My Father who is in heaven. But whoever denies Me before men, him I will also deny before My Father who is in heaven" (Matthew 10:32–33). Such reinforces the conclusion that there is a fate worse than being persecuted in this world.

The Ways of the Kingdom

Jesus' favorite way of teaching the multitude was through the use of parables—stories of everyday life that portrayed an eternal truth. As such, they appeal to the imagination, even today.

"Jesus went out of the house and sat by the sea. And great multitudes were gathered together to Him, so that He got into a boat and sat; and the whole multitude stood on the shore. Then He spoke many things to them in parables, saying: 'Behold, a sower went out to sow. And as he sowed, some seed fell by the wayside; and the birds came and devoured them. Some fell on stony places, where they did not have much earth; and they immediately sprang up because they had no depth of earth. But when the sun was up they were scorched, and because they had no root they withered away. And some fell among thorns, and the thorns sprang up and choked them. But others fell on good ground and yielded a crop:

some a hundred-fold, some sixty, some thirty. He who has ears to hear, let him hear!'" (Matthew 13:1–9).

The imagery would have been familiar to His audience, but the disciples were slow to understand why He spoke in such terms. They asked him, "'Why do You speak to them in parables?' He said to them, 'Because it has been given to you to know the mysteries of the kingdom of heaven, but to them it has not been given. For whoever has, to him more will be given, and he will have abundance; but whoever does not have, even what he has will be taken away from him. Therefore I speak to them in parables, because seeing they do not see, and hearing they do not hear, nor do they understand. And in them the prophecy of Isaiah is fulfilled, which says: "Hearing you will hear and shall not understand, And seeing you will see and not perceive; For the hearts of this people have grown dull. Their ears are hard of hearing, And their eyes they have closed, Lest they should see with their eyes and hear with their ears, lest they should understand with their hearts and turn, so that I should heal them."'" (13:10–15).

There is little agreement about the location of Matthew's primary foreign missions, but most early writers agree that he worked extensively in regions just south of the Caspian Sea.

—*Legend*

After this, Jesus went on to explain the meaning of the parable of the sower. "When anyone hears the word of the kingdom, and does not understand it, then the wicked one comes and snatches away what was sown in his heart. This is he who received seed by the wayside. But he who received the seed on stony places, this is he who hears the Word and immediately receives it with joy; yet he has no root in himself, but endures only for a while. For when tribulation or persecution arises because of the Word, immediately he stumbles. Now he who received seed among the thorns is he who hears the Word, and the cares of this world and the deceitfulness of riches choke the Word, and he becomes unfruitful. But he who received seed on the good ground is he who hears the Word and understands it, who indeed bears fruit and produces: some a hundredfold, some sixty, some thirty" (Matthew 13:19–23). Jesus went on to tell and explain more parables, most of which had to do with embracing His teachings of the kingdom, and the need for building treasure in heaven. He finally asked them, "Have you understood all these things?" (13:51). When they replied, "Yes," he continued. "Therefore every scribe instructed concerning the kingdom of heaven is like a householder who brings out of his treasure things new and old" (13:52)—he embraces both the messages that have been taught through the ages and the new ones as revealed through Jesus Christ.

In Pursuit of Excellence

The disciples subsequently inquired of Jesus: "Who then is greatest in the kingdom of heaven?" (Matthew 18:1). At this, He summoned a little child and had him stand among them. "Assuredly, I say to you," He confided, "unless you are converted and become as little children, you will by no means enter the kingdom of heaven. Therefore whoever humbles himself as this little child is the greatest in the kingdom of heaven. Whoever receives one little child like this in My name receives Me" (18:3–4).

"What do you think?" Jesus asked. "If a man has a hundred sheep, and one of them goes astray, does he not leave the ninety-nine and go to the mountains to seek the one that is straying? And if he should find it, assuredly, I say to you, he rejoices more over that sheep than over the ninety-nine that did not go astray" (Matthew 18:12–13). In like manner, "it is not the will of your Father who is in heaven that one of these little ones should perish" (18:14).

Jesus goes on to explain the nature of forgiveness, and why it adds to the growth of excellence in the spirit, by telling the parable concerning a king who wanted to settle accounts with his servants. A certain servant was unable to pay and begged for clemency. His master took pity on him, and canceled his debt. Shortly thereafter, the servant found a person who owed him a much more modest amount, and had him cast into prison. "You wicked servant," his master rebuked him. "I forgave you all that debt because you begged me. Should you not also have had compassion on your fellow servant, just as I had pity on you?" He consequently turned the man over to the jailers until he should pay back all that he owed. Jesus concluded by saying, "So My heavenly Father also will do to you if each of you, from his heart, does not forgive his brother his trespasses" (18:32–35).

The Future from the Present

Jesus had left the temple and was walking away when His disciples called His attention to a building complex. "Do you not see all these things?" He asked. "Assuredly, I say to you, not one stone shall be left here upon another, that shall not be thrown down" (Matthew 24:2).

As he was sitting on the Mount of Olives, the disciples came to Him privately. "Tell us," they implored Him, "when will these things be? And what will be the sign of Your coming, and of the end of the age?" (24:3). It was obvious that they linked the destruction of the temple with the consummation of the age. Jesus went about the task of distinguishing between the two and elaborating on each.

Chapter Eight

Jesus warned His disciples about those who would attempt to deceive them. "All these things must come to pass," He assured them, "but the end is not yet. For nation will rise against nation, and kingdom against kingdom. And there will be famines, pestilences, and earthquakes in various places. All these are the beginning of sorrows" (Matthew 24:6–8).

"Then they will deliver you up to tribulation and kill you," He continued, "and you will be hated by all nations for My name's sake, and you will be hated by all nations because of Me . . . And because lawlessness will abound, the love of many will grow cold. But he who endures to the end shall be saved. And this gospel of the kingdom will be preached in all the world as a witness to all the nations, and then the end will come" (24:9–14).

"But of that day and hour no one knows," Jesus confided, "not even the angels of heaven, but My Father only" (24:36).

"Watch therefore," He said finally, "for you do not know what hour your Lord is coming" (24:42).

After this, Jesus elaborates on the judgment to come. "All the nations will be gathered before Him, and He will separate them one from another, as a shepherd divides his sheep from the goats. And He will set the sheep on His right hand, but the goats on the left. Then the King will say to those on His right hand, 'Come, you blessed of My Father, inherit the kingdom prepared for you from the foundation of the world: for I was hungry and you gave Me food; I was thirsty and you gave Me drink; I was a stranger and you took Me in; I was naked and you clothed Me; I was sick and you visited Me; I was in prison and you came to Me.'

"Then the righteous will answer Him, saying, 'Lord, when did we see You hungry and feed You, or thirsty and give You drink? When did we see You a stranger and take You in, or naked and clothe You? Or when did we see You sick, or in prison, and come to You?' And the King will answer and say to them, 'Assuredly, I say to you, inasmuch as you did it to one of the least of these My brethren, you did it to Me.'

"Then He will also say to those on the left hand, 'Depart from Me, you cursed, into the everlasting fire prepared for the devil and his angels (Matthew 25:32–41) . . . Assuredly, I say to you, inasmuch as you did not do it to one of the least of these, you did not do it to Me.' And these will go away into everlasting punishment, but the righteous into eternal life" (25:45–46).

So Jesus alleged, and so the Gospel of Matthew assures all believers will come to pass.

The Name of Matthew

What makes Matthew unique in the Gospels is the huge contrast between the distinctive Jewishness and honor of his given name of Levi, which ironically means "connected" or "attached," and the hostile dishonor and ostracism aimed at him for his profession, which was perceived by all of Israel as traitorous. The perplexing readiness of this cynical and prosperous outcast to leave all and follow Jesus when called is understandable if we suspect that the absent honor that should go with his name is the one thing about which Levi is most cynical. Pharisees would have regarded Levi as unclean for his dealings with the Romans. Thus, merely being addressed by a renowned holy teacher and healer, let alone called to follow, probably inspired irresistible curiosity. But then, the unthinkable occurred when Jesus willingly dined with Levi and his colleagues. In retrospect, this could have been disarming in the extreme, leaving Levi with a new birth of desire or at least reheated regrets (Matthew 9:10; Mark 2:14–15; Luke 5:27–29). The Gospels imply that he immediately followed Jesus, but we are left to perceive the obvious hunger in the outcast's heart and the hope that Jesus wisely offered him.

The further glory and humor of it is that Levi, the hated, tax collecting burden upon the Hebrews, became the Spirit-anointed, God-called minister to the Hebrews, author of the first book of the New Testament and reputed "Gospel to the Hebrews," and martyr to the cause of Christ's kingdom named Matthew, which means gift of God.

The obvious lesson to us about Matthew is that no one is hopelessly outcast or without honor who follows Christ.

Apostolic Symbols and Patronages of Matthew

Matthew is represented in art as a young man, a winged man, or an angel sometimes holding a pen, inkwell, moneybag or box, purse, or to commemorate his death, a halberd, spear, lance, or sword.

Matthew's patronage is linked to:

- Ω Tax collectors and accountants
- Ω Bankers
- Ω Bookkeepers
- Ω Customs officers
- Ω Guards and security forces
- Ω Managers

Memorials

21 September (Western church)
16 November (Eastern church)

Where to Find Matthew in the Bible[9]

Ω Matthew 9:9	Tax gatherer
Ω Matthew 9:9	Becomes Christ's follower
Ω Matthew 10:2, 3	Appointed an apostle
Ω Mark 2:14	Called Levi, the son of Alphaeus

Matthew

Ω Mark 2:14, 15	Entertains Jesus with a great feast
Ω Acts 1:13	In the Upper Room
Ω Matthew 1:1	Author of the first Gospel

Chapter Nine
Thomas

Then, the same day at evening, being the first day of the week, when the doors were shut where the disciples were assembled, for fear of the Jews, Jesus came and stood in the midst, and said to them, "Peace be with you." When He had said this, He showed them His hands and

His side. Then the disciples were glad when they saw the Lord. So Jesus said to them again, "Peace to you! As the Father has sent Me, I also send you." And when He had said this, He breathed on them, and said to them, "Receive the Holy Spirit. If you forgive the sins of any, they are forgiven them; if you retain the sins of any, they are retained."

Now Thomas, called the Twin, one of the twelve, was not with them when Jesus came. The other disciples therefore said to him, "We have seen the Lord." So he said to them, "Unless I see in His hands the print of the nails, and put my finger into the print of the nails, and put my hand into His side, I will not believe." And after eight days His disciples were again inside, and Thomas with them. Jesus came, the doors being shut, and stood in the midst, and said, "Peace to you!" Then He said to Thomas, "Reach your finger here, and look at My hands; and reach your hand here, and put it into My side. Do not be unbelieving, but believing." And Thomas answered and said to Him, "My Lord and my God!" Jesus said to him, "Thomas, because you have seen Me, you have believed. Blessed are those who have not seen and yet have believed."

John 20:19–29

Although he will be perpetually committed to memory for his doubts, Thomas was, in fact, a man of great devotion, immense faith, and loyalty to God. More importantly, John—and Jesus—chose him as a messenger of one of the greatest themes in the Bible: the deity of Christ.

Very little is known about Thomas before he was chosen to be one of the twelve disciples. He was a rational, melancholy man, also known as "Didymus," which means twin. He is seen in the Gospels as the one who was most likely to assume the worst or worry about what he didn't understand.

> Historical and legendary accounts as well as local consensus all honor the apostle Thomas with the beginnings of Christianity in the southern Indian state of Kerala.
>
> —*Legend*

Some commentators have suggested that he might be the twin brother of Matthew, because of his paring with the author of the first Gospel in the lists of the apostles (Matthew 10:3; Mark 3:18; Luke 6:15). Thomas was Jewish, and although one tradition holds that he was a carpenter and builder from the area around Antioch, a city of Pisidia in Asia Minor, this seems unlikely given the attested Galilean character of the apostles. The one exception is Judas (see page 127). However, as is the case with many believers who find their lives and minds completely changed by their relationship with Christ, Thomas's past is much less important than his actions, words, and thoughts as a follower of Jesus.

While he is listed as one of the twelve by all three synoptic

Gospels, only in John is his true character revealed, when Scripture exposes him as a man who was seriously interested in all that Jesus could teach him and was so devoted to his Lord that he was willing to die with Him. While various other motivations were in place for other disciples who followed Jesus, it seems what Thomas wanted most was to understand the truth to a point where he could believe without his mind or hesitant faith interfering. What is extraordinarily special about Thomas, though, is the presence of true faith that didn't come easy for him.

> A certain place near a pond, high on the mountain of Malayattoor has been revered as the place where Thomas prayed in seclusion on his knees. The sunken marks of his knees are even suggested in a certain rock near an ancient church that has become a famous pilgrimage site.
>
> —*Legend*

Thomas first speaks out following the death of Lazarus (John 11). When Jesus speaks of returning to Bethany, which was a small town just outside of Jerusalem, Thomas turns to his fellow disciples and exhorts, "Let us also go, that we may die with Him" (11:16). The "Him" in his sentence clearly means Jesus (not Lazarus) and may refer to the fact that during other visits to the area, there had been several attempts on Jesus' life (7:1, 19, 25; 8:37, 40, 59; 10:31, 39). Although Thomas later reveals that he doesn't quite grasp everything Jesus was trying to teach His followers (John 14), there is no question regarding his devotion to Christ, even if it meant facing the threat of death.

That Thomas earnestly sought to understand the words of

Jesus becomes obvious in John 14, when the disciples are gathered in the Upper Room for the Last Supper. Jesus speaks to them of the many mansions in His Father's house, and He explains that He is going ahead to prepare a place for those who love and follow Him. Thomas, listening closely but not comprehending, probes Jesus for a better explanation of where He is going, "Lord, we do not know where You are going, and how can we know the way?" (v. 5). Since many of Jesus' followers still had in mind an earthly kingdom and a military victory, Thomas may have expected a clarification far more earth-bound than he received. As Matthew Henry points out, "Had Thomas understood, as he might have done, that Christ was going to the invisible world, the world of spirits, to which spiritual things only have a reference, he would not have said, Lord, we do not know the way."

> A unique concentration of Christianity resides in a portion of southern India where seven ancient churches attributed to Thomas still thrive.
>
> —*Legend*

Instead, Jesus' response is one of the most often quoted statements in the Bible and an essential part of Christian belief. It is the sixth "I am" statement in John, and it summarizes the core of Jesus' teaching. Jesus used Thomas' honest and open inquisitiveness to reveal a vital truth when He said simply, "I am the way, the truth, and the life. No one comes to the Father except through Me" (John 14:6). The truth is clear: Jesus is the only path to God, the only Way to true life, and only belief in Him as God Incarnate leads to salvation.

This is also the message that is carried through and underlined by Christ's final exchange with Thomas, which takes place after His Resurrection.

After the amazing news had spread about the empty tomb, all the disciples, except Thomas, had gathered together. Jesus, passing through closed and locked doors, appeared to them and gave them a blessing of peace. Yet this was not a spirit, but the living, breathing Christ, who showed the disciples the wounds in His hands and sides to let them know that the things they had heard were true.

No one knows why Thomas was absent from the group in the Upper Room. Perhaps he had stayed away because of illness or fear. Perhaps God had chosen him, because of his innate skepticism and inquisitiveness, to stay away, knowing that Thomas was the one most likely to disbelieve the account of the other disciples when they told him what had happened. In any case, God fully intended to put his absence to effective use.

Rational and perhaps forlorn souls like Thomas usually need for things to be fully comprehensible before they can commit. When Jesus died, Thomas must have felt, at first, that he had nothing to grasp. His will to follow Jesus rested on Jesus alone, what he believed and understood of Him, and what he seemed to have needed from Him. It was enough for the other apostles to be together and lean on each other in that crisis moment, but Thomas must have been more disappointed than all the others, because he dared to believe and commit in opposition to his nature. He was completely alone. Even when he finally joined the others, his doubtful rant seems more of a cry from a broken heart unwilling to be hurt again, than that of a stubborn will. Regardless of the reason, Thomas' absence set the stage for one of the most important declarations of Christ's deity in the New Testament.

Chapter Nine

Thomas did not accept the story that Christ had appeared among them. The disciples eagerly told Thomas what they had seen just as believers today share their faith and the work of God in their lives in order to build up others. Thomas, however, wanted to see for himself what the others said they had witnessed: the wounds in His sides and hands. "Unless I see in His hands the print of the nails, and put my finger into the print of the nails, and put my hand into His side, I will not believe" (John 20:25).

Numerous legends agree that Thomas was slain with a spear. He was buried on a mountain and remained there for an unknown period until his remains were taken to Edessa. Some eight hundred years later, surviving relics were transported, but the location is disputed by the Roman and eastern churches, as well as the Syriac Christians on the Malabar Coast of India.

—*Legend*

Eight days later, Thomas' longing was fulfilled. Again, the apostles were together when Christ appeared and greeted them warmly. Then He turned to Thomas in such a way that it seemed this was exactly why He had come. He acknowledged His disciple's doubt, signifying that He knew everything, even to the very words Thomas had spoken. "Then He said to Thomas, 'Reach your finger here, and look at My hands; and reach your hand here, and put it into My side. Do not be unbelieving, but believing'" (John 20:27). Jesus was merciful to Thomas' weakness and met him at the place of his anguish. The love and assurance from Jesus, as He offered to Thomas the evidence of His wounds, broke Thomas' disbelief into a flood of faith. The brokenness, humility, and surrender that the doubter offered to his beloved, lost Lord is one of the most beautiful moments in the Bible as Thomas was overcome by Christ's presence and the awesome evidence that the promise of His return (John 16:22) had been fulfilled. Thomas did not have to touch Jesus; he saw and believed, proclaiming Christ's deity as no other apostle ever did: "My Lord and my God!" (20:28).

This moment both summarizes the main theme of John's narrative and brings his Gospel to a climax of true faith and understanding. Christ acknowledges Thomas's belief—"Thomas, because you have seen Me, you have believed"—but gives encouragement to those who believe without physical evidence. Thus, the man who doubted most receives the message that will carry God's Word throughout the world—"Blessed are those who have not seen and yet have believed" (20:29).

Although Thomas' doubts have brought much ridicule to his name, those doubts served an imperative purpose in the work of Christ on this earth. Jesus used Thomas' disbelief to answer the doubts that people would have in the ages to come. As Augustine once stated, "He doubted so that we might believe."

Pope Gregory the Great would be even more vehement about the role that Thomas played. In one of his sermons, he declared:

> Do you really believe that it was by chance that this chosen disciple was absent, then came and heard, heard and doubted, doubted and touched, touched and believed? It was not by chance but in God's providence. In a marvelous way God's mercy arranged that the disbelieving disciple, in touching the wounds of his master's body, should heal our wounds of

> disbelief. The disbelief of Thomas has done more for our faith than the faith of the other disciples. As he touches Christ and is won over to belief, every doubt is cast aside and our faith is strengthened. So the disciple who doubted, then felt Christ's wounds, becomes a witness to the reality of the Resurrection.

After this historically significant moment, John winds down his account of Christ as Lord with His appearance to the disciples at the seashore, where He cooked for them, blessed them with an overwhelming catch of fish, and instructed them to follow Him for the remainder of their lives. The gentle apostle Thomas was at hand, and according to tradition, never again doubted the immutable Word of the Lord.

Apostolic Symbols and Patronages of Thomas

Thomas is symbolized by the spear of his martyrdom or a carpenter's square pointing to the legend that he built a palace for a king in India.

Thomas' patronage includes:

- Struggle against doubt
- Architects, builders, stone masons
- Blind people
- Geometricians, theologians
- The nations of India, Pakistan, Sri Lanka, and Ceylon East Indies

Memorials

3 July (Western church)
6 October (Eastern church)

Where to Find Thomas in the Bible[9]

Ω Matthew 10:3, Mark 3:18	Apostle of Christ
Ω John 11:16	Ready to die with Christ
Ω John 14:1–6	In need of instruction
Ω John 20:19–24	Not present when Christ appears
Ω John 20:25	States terms of belief
Ω John 20:26–29, John 21:1, 2	Christ appears before Thomas
Ω Acts 1:13	In the Upper Room

Chapter Ten
James, Son of Alphaeus

Then they returned to Jerusalem from the mount called Olivet, which is near Jerusalem, a Sabbath day's journey. And when they had entered, they went up into the upper room where they were staying: Peter, James, John, and Andrew; Philip and Thomas; Bartholomew and Matthew; James the son of Alphaeus and Simon the Zealot; and Judas the son of James. These all continued with one accord in prayer and supplication, with the women and Mary the mother of Jesus, and with His brothers.

Acts 1:12–14

One of the more intriguing aspects of examining the life of this apostle is the debate about who he is not. Part of the disagreement arises because there are five different references to "James" in the New Testament, yet very little scriptural or historical evidence about whether these are actually five different men.

1. James, the brother of John, was a prominent apostle, and is profiled in another chapter of this book (see page 37).
2. James the Less, or James the Younger (Mark 15:40), who is mentioned several times in Scripture (see Matthew 27:56; Mark 16:1; Luke 24:10), and is sometimes called the son of Mary, or the brother of Joses. Some scholars believe this James is also the son of Alphaeus.
3. James, the father of Judas (Luke 6:16; Acts 1:13), is also possibly Thaddaeus.
4. James, the Lord's brother (Matthew 13:55; Mark 6:3), who is the most likely candidate to be the author of the Epistle of James, and who later became a church leader in Jerusalem (see Acts 12:17; 15:13; 21:18). While a number of people, including Jerome, have argued that this is also the son of Alphaeus, there is no definitive proof of this.
5. James, the son of Alphaeus, who is mentioned by this name only four times in the Bible (Matthew 10:3; Mark 3:18; Luke 6:15; Acts 1:13).

Whatever background or history exists within the first-century church, James was more than the son of Alphaeus—he was also a child of God. As one of the twelve apostles, he would have been a man of devotion and love, of deep faith, and extensive spiritual gifts. Along with the others, he would have heard the Good News of salvation directly from Jesus Christ, and he would have been commissioned to carry that message to all nations of the world. So many doubts about his identity remain, but there can be no doubt about his purpose in life.

The James Enigma

How should we, then, remember the pillars of the early church of Christ named James? As two different men? Three? Or five?

It is generally held that, although the apostle James (son of Zebedee and brother of John) is clearly distinct among the first four disciples of the Lord, tradition has identified the apostle, James the Less, with James the Just (the Lord's brother or cousin), who became the bishop of the Jerusalem church. Much commentary about James the Less is based on this very presumption. This is reasonable, but it may also be motivated by the desire to attribute the parents of James the Less, Alphaeus and Mary, to those of Bishop James as well, in order to call him a cousin of the Lord instead of a brother.

> The writing of the early church historians from Josephus to Eusebius universally attribute the traditions of James the Less with the Bishop of Jerusalem, who was the Lord's brother.
>
> —*Legend*

Many Catholic and Orthodox scholars support this answer when the purity of Mary is challenged.

Scholars of more recent times dispute the two-James presumption, however, for numerous textual and historical reasons.

If the Lord's own brother, or cousin, had been a disciple, Jesus would likely have called him to his familial duty to care for Mary, rather than John (John 19:25–27). To his own peril, John had shown himself to be relationally the closest to Mary and singularly faithful by supporting her at her Son's execution.

It is also regarded as unlikely that James, the Lord's brother, would readily become such a committed disciple after standing with his brethren who repudiated him (7:1–9).

Something dramatic must have happened to transform James into a man self-abandoned and committed enough to the lost sheep of Israel, that even the most ascetic among the Essenes and Pharisees called him James the Just.

Paul records a private appearance of the resurrected Jesus to James after, and distinct from, His appearance to "the twelve" (1 Corinthians 15:5, 7). Paul also refers to James as an apostle (Galatians 1:18, 19), likewise with Silas and Timothy (1 Thessalonians 1:1, 2:6). But unlike Paul and Peter, both James and his brother Jude, refer to themselves only as servants of the Lord Jesus Christ (James 1:1; Jude 1:1).

In the eastern world, it was not uncommon for the brother of one who died to take up the cause of the fallen one. Besides His calling to be the Lamb of God for the world, Jesus came personally to seek and save the lost sheep of Israel. That Jesus would visit James, later ordained bishop of Jerusalem and pastor of all the Jewish church, privately, would seem divinely harmonious with seeing him as the Lord's heir to his first mission. It also provides the needed "Damascus Road" epiphany to explain the dramatic contrast between James the Scoffer (Mark 3:21) and James the Just, who also wrote the Epistle of James.

Alas if, indeed, the Bishop of Jerusalem was a third James, then we know nothing of fact about James the Less—except that he was numbered among the twelve who are listed in the Gospels as original apostles, and that his father's name was Alphaeus.

No other mention of him is given in the New Testament. He would be uniquely anonymous without even sufficient conjecture about him, except that since Matthew's father was named Alphaeus as well, the two could have been brothers. This seems an untenable silence about an apostle ordained by the Lord.

There is vague historical evidence within Jewish tradition that James the Less was martyred in Egypt by the Jews who accused him of violating the Law of Moses. Any solid evidence for this or other contrasting end for James the Less would put to rest his relation with James the Just.

It may very well be that James the Less should now be remembered by that title, not because he was younger or perhaps smaller, but because, among the twelve whom the Lord called to change the world, his labor was done in the greatest obscurity and yet may be the most honored (Matthew 6:2–4). If, however, the barely mentioned apostle, James the Less, became the highly honored Shaliach of the Lord's mission to the lost sheep of Israel and chief servant of Judaic Christians, and an author of Scripture, then this too would be divine harmony with the humorously unpredictable and ironic ways that God reveals Himself in the lives of His servants.

Apostolic Symbols and Patronages of James the Less

James the Less is represented by a man holding a book or a fullers club. The latter attests the identity of James the Less with James, the Lord's brother.

James' patronage is linked to:

- The dying
- Apothecaries

- Fullers
- Millers
- Hat makers

Memorial

3 May

Where to Find James the Less in the Bible[9]

Matthew 10:3, 4	Son of Alphaeus; one of the twelve
Mark 15:40	Identified usually as "the Less"
Matthew 27:56	Brother of Joses

Chapter Eleven
Jude Thaddaeus

Jesus said to the apostles, "If you love Me, keep My commandments. And I will pray the Father, and He will give you another Helper, that He may abide with you forever—the Spirit of truth . . . you know Him, for He dwells with you and will be in you. He who has My commandments and keeps them, it is he who loves Me. And he who loves Me will be loved by My Father, and I will love him and manifest Myself to him." And Jude said to Him, "Lord, how is it that You will manifest Yourself to us, and not to the world?"

John 14:15–22

The apostle, Jude Thaddaeus, has always been something of an enigma for lack of tangible information in the Bible before he became one of Christ's chosen disciples. Some reports indicate that he was born in a village called Paneas, which was later renamed Caesarea Philippi. He may have been a fisherman or a farmer. What is reasonably assumed about his heritage is that he was the son or brother of James (Luke 6:13). But for the most part, Jude Thaddaeus carried on his apostolic duties without much fanfare or notoriety prior to the Ascension.

Jude was probably best known as the apostle with three names: Judas, Thaddaeus, and Lebbaeus. Thaddaeus comes from the Aramaic term "Theudus," which means breast, chest, or heart. Lebbaeus may derive from the Hebrew noun "leb" which means the heart. Both are terms of endearment and were probably given to him as a young boy by someone who cared deeply for him. Judas (or Jude), which means praise or giver of joy, was his given name, and was one of the most common male names among Jews of Bible times. There are two other prominent figures in the Bible who share this name: Judas Iscariot; and Jude, the "brother" of Jesus, who was likely the author of the Epistle of Jude.

In Acts 1:13, he is again known as Judas, son of James, possibly to distinguish him from Judas Iscariot, the traitor. That is specifically noted in John 14:22, when Jude posed his earnest question to his Savior.

As noted, Jude Thaddaeus was the son of James, but much uncertainty exists regarding which James was his father, as there were several prominent men named James in the Bible. It is not likely that he was the son of fellow apostle, James, son of Alphaeus, because this James was also called "James the Less," which may have denoted him to be a younger man, making him closer in age to Jude. If a family tree and historical literature are any indication, then James the Less would have been Jude's older brother. And since their mother, Mary, was the blood sister of Mary, the mother of Jesus, they would have been first cousins of Jesus. Jude's mother was the Mary who stood at the foot of the Cross and then anointed Jesus' body after His death.

In another, less likely scenario, it was assumed that Jude Thaddaeus was the son of James of Zebedee (or "James the Great"), who was also a beloved apostle of Christ. If this were the correct assumption, then Jude would have been the grandson of Zebedee and Salome. Salome was reportedly another sister of Jesus' mother, Mary, and this would have ultimately made Jude Thaddaeus a more distant cousin of Jesus.

> Relics of the apostle with three names can reportedly be found in three cities—Rome, Rheims, and Toulouse, France.
>
> —*Legend*

Granted, it is mostly conjecture, but whether or not he was a relative of Jesus, Jude must have been honored to be a part of His circle of apostles—the chosen few who would know Him intimately and personally, learning from Him so that they could march into history as those who would spread His gospel—those who would carry on the Shaliach tradition.

The permanent office of Apostleship is the cloak of headship in the church, which eleven of the closest disciples later received when the Spirit anointed the church on Pentecost.

As in Matthew 10:2, the twelve, including Iscariot, are referred to in the Gospels as "Apostles" when they were sent out two-by-two to preach and heal, thus tasting briefly the calling they would soon be given.

Jude Thaddaeus

It is understandable that none of the twelve, and certainly none of the other numerous disciples, even remotely had a grasp on the future. To be sure, they were humbled afterward. Paul called himself the chief of sinners and wondered that he, of all people, would be called to preach to the Gentiles.

> Jude traveled and preached in Judea, Idumaea, Syria, Mesopotamia, Lybia, and especially Armenia, which, in the third century, grew into the first Christian nation.
>
> —*Legend*

As for Jude's calling, he was chosen by Christ for reasons not known to us. He guided him in ways not revealed to us. And Jude Thaddaeus was a paradigm of His abounding grace. But no matter how little is actually known about him, Jude Thaddaeus is recorded in perpetual history for the only question attributed to him in the entire Bible. In that question, one can hear the overtures of a Shaliach calling. Jesus' response to Jude's question was one of seed comfort—words that the apostles would soon recall and never forget in times of fear and persecution.

Jesus said, "If anyone loves Me, he will keep My word; and My Father will love him, and We will come to Him and make Our home with Him. He who does not love Me does not keep My words; and the word which you hear is not Mine but the Father's who sent Me.

"These things I have spoken to you while being present with you. But the Helper, the Holy Spirit, whom the Father will send in My name, He will teach you all things, and bring to your remembrance all things that I said to you. Peace I leave with you, My peace I give to you; not as the world gives do I give to you. Let not your heart be troubled, neither let it be afraid" (John 14:23–27).

Chapter Eleven

Jude Thaddaeus joined eleven others on a wonderful journey that could have taken him anywhere, but he needed to know that the rest of creation would know Jesus. Even at the risk of losing everything, including his life, he was concerned about the people of the world hearing the message of the gospel. In that question, Jude seemed to be asking for his own role in the Great Commission to begin. And in that question, he seemed to know that he would be one of the twelve who would change the world. His tenderness and perhaps youthful idealism motivated him to want the world to know Jesus, but he knew little to nothing of the gospel at this point.

This little drama between Jude, who would be sent, and Jesus, who was sent and now sends, overtures well with the Shaliach principle—the One who is sent is as the one who sends. He does God's work. He speaks on God's behalf. And the Christian world is indebted to Jude Thaddaeus for his apostolic role in Christian ministry.

> Jude was ordered executed by the Armenian King Sanatrouk, the son of Abgar's sister, for baptizing his daughter into Christ.
>
> —*Legend*

Jude's bold question—perhaps his only words in the Bible unless he was also the author of the Epistle of Jude—was answered by the Lord with encouragement for faithful followers who love Him (John 14:23, 24). But it was also answered providentially through Jude's later missionary work in Mesopotamia and Armenia. It is important to note that, in the third century, Armenia became the first heathen nation to officially declare itself Christian.

Jude Thaddaeus

Saint Jude is the patron of hopeless and impossible causes, and there are tales of cures and acts of grace bestowed upon people who turn to St. Jude. It will never be known whether these are miracles or coincidences. However, it is known that St. Jude is the symbol and crucible of hope for many Christians. Were it not for hope, the human heart would break. Hope is one of the great spiritual virtues. It is remembering what God has already done in history and what God has promised to do in the future. Hope is the realization that the love of God has permanently affected humankind—that the whole of creation will eventually be lifted up to God. "And we know that all things work together for good to those who love God, to those who are the called according to His purpose" (Romans 8:28).

Jude, likely the youngest of the twelve, asks the seminal question of the prenatal church and, according to Eusebius, was probably the first to complete a personal mission to carry Christ's healing and Baptism to others outside of the lost sheep of Israel. The historian quite fervently believed the accounts he uncovered in the Edessa (now Sanliurfa, in modern Turkey) archives and retold in his first book of church history of the healing and baptism of its King Abgar.

The fame of Jesus' miracles and healing work must have spread to Asia Minor. The suffering Abgar sent emissaries with a letter to entreat Jesus to come to him. Eusebius apparently held the letter and its response from Jesus in his hand. Little, if any, historical authentication is given to the now absent documents. The account states that the Lord blessed Abgar for believing in Him though he had not seen Him. Jesus then promised to send one of His disciples to bring healing and life to Abgar and his household after He had finished His work and returned to the One who had sent Him. Legend has it that it was Jude Thaddeus who was sent and performed all that was promised. The King was converted and then commanded a great assembly of the people and nobles to hear Jude's preaching.

Other apostles also labored for the advancement of the gospel in eastern Asia Minor and Persia after Jude had apparently opened the first doors. Jude is believed to have been martyred expanding his work in present-day northern Iran and buried near Tabriz.

But if the legend which Eusebius recorded about the letter and healing of King Abgar of Edessa is even remotely true, it means that Jude answered his own question on a mission to heathens, which the Lord Himself may have commissioned before His death. The poetic justice of it is remarkable and very much like the humor of our God.

The Name of Jude Thaddaeus

Jude Thaddaeus was probably called Jude, rather than Judah or Judas, out of special care to protect him from confusion with the traitor. The name Judah is a confession of praise to God. Thaddaeus means "breast" or "heart," and Lebbaeus means "man of heart." The names ring true in the praiseworthy longings and deeds of Jude and the absence of any recorded rebuke of him from Jesus. They infer an unhesitating faithfulness lived out of a noble heart.

Apostolic Symbols and Patronages of Jude Thaddaeus

Jude is symbolized as a fisherman or a bearded man holding an oar, a boat or boat hook, a club, an axe, or a book.

His patronage is linked to:

- Impossible and hopeless causes
- Desperate situations

- Hospital workers and hospitals
- Diocese of Saint Petersburg, FL

Memorials

28 October (Western church)
19 June (Eastern church)

Where to Find Jude Thaddaeus in the Bible[9]

Mark 3:18	One of the twelve apostles
Matthew 10:3	Surnamed Thaddaeus
Luke 6:13, 16	One of Christ's apostles
John 14:22	Asks Jesus a question
Acts 1:13	Son of James

Chapter Twelve
Simon the Zealot

Now it came to pass in those days that He went out to the mountain to pray, and continued all night in prayer to God. And when it was day, He called His disciples to Himself; and from them He chose twelve whom He also named apostles: Simon, whom He also named Peter, and Andrew his brother; James and John; Philip and Bartholomew; Matthew and Thomas; James the son of Alphaeus, and Simon called the Zealot; Judas the son of James, and Judas Iscariot who also became a traitor.

Luke 6:12–16

Simon, along with a number of the other apostles, is known only for being a chosen apostle of Jesus. He's listed only four times (Matthew 10:4; Mark 3:18; Luke 6:15; Acts 1:13), yet his impact on the growth of the young church must have been great, due to both his gifts as an apostle and his enthusiasm as a zealot.

> Ancient but unproven histories such as the Martyrologies of St. Jerome, Bede, Ado and Usard agree that the Persian mission work of Simon led to his death.
>
> —*Legend*

Simon is referred to as "the Canaanite" by Matthew (10:4) and Mark (3:18) and "a Zealot" by Luke (6:15; Acts 1:13), probably to distinguish him initially from Peter, who was also called Simon. Yet the two terms also give a clue about both Simon's background and his personality.

Matthew and Mark's reference to Simon as a "Canaanite" or "Cananite" probably means that he grew up in the village of Cana in Galilee. That was the site of Jesus' first public miracle: the changing of water into wine at a wedding (John 2:1–11). One tradition claims that Simon was the bridegroom at that wedding, and his witness to the miracle persuaded him to follow Jesus. While this story is certainly romantic, it is also apocryphal.

Some modern translations have dropped the "Canaanite" reference, however, using "Zealot" in all four listings, which emphasizes his fervent dedication to his faith. The Zealots were a sect of Jews who were fanatical about their faith, as well as their politics. They were completely dedicated to God and His Law, and they were willing to fight for Him. Many scholars believe his being called "the Zealot" means, as the Aramaic "gan'anai" would suggest, that Simon was, indeed, a partisan within one of the groups of proud, orthodox separatists who were collectively, and somewhat derogatorily referred to as zealots. Others refute this, pointing out that the infamous Zealot rebellion didn't begin until a few years before the destruction of Jerusalem. It is true that some factions of these purists didn't become violent and infamous until many years later, but the fervently anti-Hellenistic, zealot counter-culture is known to have existed almost from the beginning of the Roman occupation.

One legend holds that Simon and the apostle, Jude, became angry with pagan priests, much like Jesus in the Temple, and overturned their idol statues. The priests retaliated, and had Simon and Jude imprisoned and tortured before they died.

—*Legend*

They were violently opposed to the Roman rule of Palestine, and their dedication eventually led to a revolt in A.D. 66, and the destruction of Jerusalem in A.D. 70. The last of the Zealots fled to Masada, in the Idumea region near the Dead Sea, where they staged a standoff against the Romans that is one of the most well-known battles in history.

In other words, this was not a sect that was taken lightly, and a man who was called a Zealot would have been seen as a fiery, indomitable messenger of God's Word. He would not have hesitated when Jesus instructed His apostles to go and share the message of salvation with the world. Both scripture and legend seem to uphold

Simon as a just man whose devotion to the purity of the Mosaic tradition was not tainted by greed, political pride, or personal ambition, unlike Judas Iscariot.

In the apocryphal "Acts of Andrew," an ancient tomb rests in a Persian province that claims to be the site where Simon the Zealot was interred.

—*Legend*

If the legend of Simon's zeal against idols, mentioned in the Legends section on page 124, is true, it reveals something of the relationship Simon had with Christ. No doubt all the apostles, especially Simon, fulfilled the same spirit prophesied about Christ and fulfilled in Jesus when He overturned the money changing tables and unjust weights in the Temple. Then His disciples remembered that it was written, "Zeal for Your house has eaten Me up"(John 2:17; Psalm 69:9). Whether the story gave rise to the name or the name gave rise to the story is presently uncertain. Either way, a pure hearted, zealous nature is presumed about Simon.

The most horrifically detailed account of Simon's martyrdom claims that he was tied down to a wagon wheel while two men cut through his body lengthwise with a buck saw.

—*Legend*

No one is sure what became of Simon after the anointing of the Holy Spirit in the Upper Room (Acts 2). One tradition says that he traveled with Jude into Persia, where they ministered to the people and were eventually killed while serving God. What is known for sure is that Jesus chose His apostles carefully and wisely, and it was their "zeal" and love for Him that helped successfully spread His message throughout the entire world.

Apostolic Symbols and Patronages of Simon the Zealot

Simon is represented in art as a man being sawn in half bi-symmetrically. His symbols are a boat, a fish or two fish, an oar, a saw, and a lance.

His patronages includes:

- Ω Curriers
- Ω Sawmen or sawyers
- Ω Tanners

Memorial

28 October

Where to Find Simon in the Bible[9]

Ω Matthew 10:4, Mark 3:18, Luke 6:15	One of the twelve; called "the Canaanite" or "the zealot"

Chapter Thirteen
Judas Iscariot

When Jesus had said these things, He was troubled in spirit, and testified and said, "Most assuredly, I say to you, one of you will betray Me." Then the disciples looked at one another, perplexed about whom He spoke. Now there was leaning on Jesus' bosom one of His disciples, whom Jesus loved. Simon Peter therefore motioned to him to ask who it was of whom He spoke. Then, leaning back on Jesus' breast, he said to Him, "Lord, who is it?" Jesus answered, "It is he to whom I shall give a piece of bread when I have dipped it." And having dipped the bread, He gave it to Judas Iscariot, the son of Simon. Now after the piece of bread, Satan entered him. Then Jesus said to him, "What you do, do quickly." But no one at the table knew for what reason He said this to him. For some thought, because Judas had the moneybox, that Jesus had said to him, "Buy those things we need for the feast," or that he should give something to the poor. Having received the piece of bread, he then went out immediately. And it was night.

John 13:21–30

It would be a great comfort to know that Judas Iscariot was, at one time in his life, a righteous and devoted man. This is an easy fact to forget about a man whose betrayal is so legendary that his name alone has become synonymous with deception and treachery. Judas, however, may not have been born evil; he may have been an innocent and simple child, before he grew to be an untarnished, young man with dreams for his future. Judas may have come by his moral collapse the same way many well-meaning believers do—he put his own desires and motivations above those of God.

Judas Iscariot's name indicates that he was from Kerioth, a city located in southern Judah, which makes Judas the only apostle who was not a Galilean. Although there is a mention of Simon, his father (John 6:71), not much else is known about Judas before Jesus called him to be one of His followers. Judas is mentioned in all three lists of the apostles in the synoptic Gospels (Matthew 10:4; Mark 3:19; Luke 6:16), but always with the label of traitor, which will be his eternally and notoriously negative legacy.

At the time of Jesus' ministry, however, the other apostles obviously trusted him—he was the treasurer for the group and made purchases for them or for people they wanted to help (see John 12:6; 13:29). He had been with them from the beginning. Like the other eleven, Judas had witnessed Jesus' works and the miraculous growth of His ministry. He sat at Jesus' feet, and he heard the message of God's salvation. How could anyone witness the miracles, see the hunger of the people for the Word, hear God's plan for His kingdom, and then just turn and walk away for thirty pieces of silver?

Some commentators have felt that the reason was simply greed: John does point out that Judas was a thief (John 12:6). Others think Judas' reasons were political, and that he believed Jesus, as the

Son of God, was going to bring a political revolution to the Jews. Impatient, Judas hoped to force Jesus into action through the betrayal. Either—or both—could be reasonable explanations.

Another theory states that Judas was becoming disillusioned with Jesus. Matthew and Mark, the two earliest accounts of Jesus' ministry, juxtapose the account of Judas' decision to go to the priests with the account of Mary's anointing Christ with oil from the alabaster box (Matthew 26:6–16; Mark 14:3–10) and the displeasure expressed by the disciples. John points out that whatever Judas' impure motives were, his heart was fully conquered by Satan. His language is blunt: "Satan entered" Judas (John 13:27) prior to his visit to the priests. Yet, whether the reason was greed, political maneuvering, or a supernatural urge, Judas still made a clear choice to betray the Son of God.

The Last Supper perfectly highlights the circumstances surrounding Judas. "Most assuredly, I say to you," Jesus confided, "one of you will betray Me" (13:21). His disciples stared at one another, at a loss to know which was implicated. "Lord," John inquired, leaning back, "who is it?" Jesus answered, "It is he to whom I shall give a piece of bread when I have dipped it" (13:25–26). After dipping the bread, he gave it to Judas Iscariot. It was customary at the conclusion of a feast for the host to take a piece of bread and "sop" up any remaining meat juice or even the last of his own wine and give it to one of his honored guests.

This has led some to suppose that Judas was reclining at the other place of honor, at Jesus' left. There is an old saying: "Keep your friends close and your enemies closer." But Jesus certainly needed no protection from Judas. It would, however, add to the condemnation of Judas to betray Jesus after He had so honored him at the table as well as having appointed him the purse keeper.

It is a plausible scenario, but John does not elaborate. The subtlety of the exchange John describes in 13:23–29 makes it appear that the remaining apostles were removed enough at the table to miss the point and its profound significance.

Judas then left the table fully committed to his objective. He may have even interpreted the Lord's honors for him and last words to him as concession to his plan. If so, imagine the enthusiasm he would have had believing the Lord was finally going to bring His great power to bare on the Romans and His enemies and usher in the true Davidic kingdom with him at His left side, no less. But he was to have his arrogance and presumption crushed.

After he betrayed Jesus with a kiss, Judas was apparently surprised to find out that Jesus had been condemned to die. Suddenly, he knew he had committed a great sin (Matthew 27:3–4). He went back to the priests and tried to rescind his deal with them, and he threw the money at their feet. When they would not release Jesus, Judas remorsefully hung himself.

Even though he had traveled for three years with a man who showed unbelievable mercy and forgiveness toward sinners, Judas did not think to ask God's forgiveness.

After Judas' death, Matthias was chosen to replace him as one of the twelve apostles. In Peter's speech to the followers of Christ, asking them to nominate two possible candidates, he points out that Judas' betrayal and death, as well as the choosing of a replacement, were the fulfillments of prophecies made in the Old Testament (Acts 1:20).

Jesus certainly knew, even as He selected the man from Kerioth as His apostle, that Judas was the one who would betray Him.

There were no predictions or foreknowledge, however, that could have forced Judas to make the choices he did. He turned his back on God of his own free will, surrendering his trust and faith to his own desires and predilections. Such is the lesson that he leaves to all believers, even today.

Chapter Thirteen

Apostolic Symbols and Patronages of Judas Iscariot

In a way Judas was a martyr to his own cause of trying to force the Lord to claim the kingdom as he understood it. He was devoted to this cause, not to Jesus. Therefore, there is no patronage associated with him and when the apostleship of Judas is symbolized, one sees a blank yellow shield. Yellow depicts his faithless heart. The blank shield depicts his fruitless discipleship.

When he is portrayed personally, he carries a moneybag or thirty pieces of silver. Sometimes he is portrayed with a rope around his neck, depicting his suicide.

Where to Find Judas Iscariot in the Bible[9]

Ω Matthew 10:4, Mark 3:19, Luke 6:16	One of the apostles
Ω John 6:71	". . . and one of you is a devil"
Ω John 12:4	Judas rebukes Jesus about the oil
Ω John 13:26	Jesus gives Judas the sop
Ω Matthew 26:14, 25, Mark 14:10, Luke 22:3, John 13:2	Judas betrays Jesus
Ω John 13:29	Apostles misunderstand Judas' intent
Ω Matthew 26:47, Mark 14:43, Luke 22:47, John 18:2–5	Judas leads the Pharisees to Jesus
Ω Matthew 26:48–49, Mark 14:44–45, Luke 22:47–48	Judas betrays Jesus with a kiss
Ω Matthew 27:3	Judas is remorseful

Beyond the Twelve: Matthias and Paul

How important is it that we include a discussion regarding Matthias and Paul in this book about the twelve original apostles? Peter and the congregation of Jerusalem clearly saw the calling of Matthias into the role of apostleship as very important, and given the abundant fruits of Paul's labors following his dramatic conversion to follow Christ, we must also mark them as important enough to include as part of this work. Matthias and Paul both received the apostolic calling into the glorious harvest that our Lord's passion and victory cultivated, and their impact on the foundation of our faith is immeasurable. We honor them here.

Matthias

Peter stood up in the midst of the disciples (altogether the number of names was about a hundred and twenty), and said, "Men and brethren, this Scripture had to be fulfilled, which the Holy Spirit spoke before by the mouth of David concerning Judas, who became a guide to those who arrested Jesus; for he was numbered with us and obtained a part in this ministry . . . Let another take his office."

"Therefore, of these men who have accompanied us all the time that the Lord Jesus went in and out among us, . . . one of these must become a witness with us of His resurrection."

And they proposed two: Joseph called Barsabas, . . . and Matthias. And they prayed and said, "You, O Lord, who know the hearts of all, show which of these two You have chosen to take part in this ministry and apostleship from which Judas by transgression fell, that he might go to his own place." And they cast their lots, and the lot fell on Matthias. And he was numbered with the eleven apostles.

Acts 1:15–18, 21–26

The name Matthias means gift of God, and the disciples of Jesus must have felt that this hard-working man was, indeed, one of God's gifts when he was chosen to replace Judas. Very little is known about Matthias, and Acts 1 features the only mention of him by name in the Bible. Yet his impact on the young church was enormous, and his election demonstrated the unity and faith of the followers of Jesus Christ.

> One legend claims that Matthias was stoned to death in Cochis (Ethiopia) in A.D. 80. Some of his remains may be in Saint Matthias' Abbey in Trier, Germany, while other relics may be in Saint Mary Major in Rome.
>
> —*Legend*

The church was still trying to find its true path for spreading the ministry of Christ at that time. Jesus had ascended, but the anointing of the Holy Spirit in the Upper Room had not yet occurred. After Judas had died, Peter went to the assembly of "men and brethren" who had been with Christ during His ministry on earth and asked them to choose someone to join with the eleven other disciples. He clearly saw this as a fulfillment of a prophecy as stated in Psalms (Acts 1:20; also see Psalm 69:25; 109:8), and Peter probably could have chosen the new apostle himself, or had the eleven others help him. Instead, he turned to the entire 120-member fellowship of disciples for their estimation.

> Matthias ministered to barbarous cannibals in Ethiopia.
>
> —*Legend*

They nominated two men, Matthias and Barsabas. Both must have been loyal and devoted, to be admired by so many, and to be chosen out of such a large fellowship. They both had been with Jesus, as Peter pointed out, from the beginning of this ministry through His Crucifixion, Resurrection, and Ascension. They had heard His message, and they had followed the other disciples as they worked, prayed, and ministered to unbelievers. With two such equal, worthy candidates in front of them, the apostles then turned to God with prayer, and the casting of lots to make the final choice.

> Another legend claims that Matthias was stoned to death by Jews in Jerusalem and then beheaded.
>
> —*Legend*

Casting lots was seen as a request for God's intervention and direction, and it was a legal way to resolve an issue. When the lot fell to Matthias, it was seen as God's ordination of him as the right choice for the ministry to which the apostles had been called. Although Matthias is not mentioned again by name, he must have been with the other apostles on that day when the Holy Spirit filled the room and empowered each of them to go out and take the words of Christ into the world. In the wake of the world's most notorious betrayal, Matthias emerged as a man called by God.

The Name of Matthias

Matthias, a shortened form of Mattathias, means "gift of God." By his name alone, it might be fitting to say that he was destined to become the apostle chosen to replace Judas Iscariot. However, Matthias' fellow disciple, with whom he was paired to cast lots for that esteemed role, was Joseph called Barsabas. And Joseph means "Jehovah has added." So, it seems that Matthias and Joseph both began fulfilling the meaning of their names when they were chosen from 120 men to vie for the one position with the brotherhood of Christ's apostles. Although little is given to Matthias in the way of written history, he was given a "gift of God" through his ability to minister and reportedly preached the gospel for over 30 years in Judea, Cappadocia, Egypt, and Ethiopia before his death.

One exciting myth surrounding Matthias holds that he was preaching in Macedonia when he was imprisoned. His captors tried to blind him, but he became invisible to them and escaped harm. The Lord then appeared to him and gave him hope until he was freed.

—Legend

Apostolic Symbols and Patronages of Matthias

Matthias is symbolized by an older man either holding or being impaled by an axe, lance, scimitar, or sword.

Another myth claims that Matthias was imprisoned by the high priest of Judea, Ananias—the same high priest who ordered the death of the apostle James. Matthias was stoned, and then decapitated by an axe.

—Legend

Matthias' patronage has been linked to:

- Ω Alcoholism and reformed alcoholics
- Ω Carpenters
- Ω Smallpox
- Ω Tailors
- Ω The Diocese of Great Falls and Billings, Montana

Memorials

9 August (Eastern church)
24 February (Western church)

Where to Find Matthias in the Bible[9]

Ω Acts 1:15	Matthias chosen to replace Judas
Ω Acts 1:23	Barbasabas and Matthias are both named
Ω Acts 1:26	The lot fell on Matthias

Paul

But the Lord said to him, "Go, for he is a chosen vessel of Mine to bear My name before Gentiles, kings, and the children of Israel. For I will show him how many things he must suffer for My name's sake." And Ananias went his way and entered the house; and laying his hands on him he said, "Brother Saul, the Lord Jesus, who appeared to you on the road as you came, has sent me that you may receive your sight and be filled with the Holy Spirit." Immediately there fell from his eyes something like scales, and he received his sight at once; and he arose and was baptized. So when he had received food, he was strengthened. Then Saul spent some days with the disciples at Damascus. Immediately he preached the Christ in the synagogues, that He is the Son of God. Then all who heard were amazed, and said, "Is this not he who destroyed those who called on this name in Jerusalem, and has come here for that purpose, so that he might bring them bound to the chief priests?" But Saul increased all the more in strength, and confounded the Jews who dwelt in Damascus, proving that this Jesus is the Christ.

Acts 9:15–22

Paul (Saul), apostle to the Gentiles, appears in Scripture as a bundle of energy. He was born and spent his childhood in Tarsus, a major population center located in the province of Cilicia (modern Turkey), in the southeastern region of Asia Minor. He was born a Roman citizen, although it is not known how his parents acquired this status. Paul was his Roman name, as was Saul his Hebrew alternative.

Paul is first encountered as a devout Pharisee and a zealous advocate of Jewish Law. In this capacity, he vigorously persecuted the followers of Jesus. Paul reports that he was mentored in the law by the esteemed teacher Gamaliel, who cautioned the authorities against persecuting the followers of Jesus, since if they were not of God they would not succeed. Conversely, if they were of God, one would not want to oppose the Almighty. Saul was not of like mind, and set out to oppress the fledgling community. He was acting out of zeal for his religious heritage. His later confession might suggest that baser motives were also involved (2 Corinthians 12:16). He perhaps saw this as an opportunity to ingratiate himself with the religious establishment.

It would seem that the thorn and all that Paul the apostle suffered for the Gospel purchased and maintained humility for him. He penned more of the New Testament than anyone else and stated that he labored more than all the apostles (1 Corinthians 15:10). He established more churches and, no doubt, performed miracles within them. His ministry enlightened the Jewish church regarding the availability of grace to the Gentiles and the efficacy of faith above law. Such a high calling would eventually poison the self-image of anyone not tethered to reality by pain, but especially so in the heart of a young and ambitious scholar. Paul was content and grateful to God for His grace. He even gloried in his need for such discipline, and that has become a lesson to us about God's strength made perfect in our weakness (2 Corinthians 12:9).

Saul was an "all or nothing" kind of a person. He would not compromise or let anyone else compromise, as Peter abruptly discovered (Galatians 2:11–13). In order for Paul to be fruitful as an "all or nothing" kind of an apostle, once his energies were redirected, he would need the continual admonitions of hard-won humility, starting with a profoundly new birth experience. His encounter with Jesus was necessary to show him his blindness and silence his arrogance. It is what Paul, referring to himself, called "born out of due time" (1 Corinthians 15:8).

Legend holds that Paul was martyred at Aquae Salviae, near Rome, but his burial place is at the Basilica of San Paolo fuori le mura.

—*Legend*

It began with the martyrdom of Stephen, to which Saul was consenting and over which he may have presided (Acts 7:55–60). As Stephen was dying, he cried out to God to forgive those who were stoning him. Notice that Stephen saw Jesus standing at the right side of the Father. Stephen's prayer on behalf of them all was a perfect echo of the forgiving love Jesus conferred upon His own executioners.

Sometime after this, an astonishing thing happened to Paul as he neared Damascus, where he intended to ferret out any Christians and bring them, bound up, to Jerusalem (9:1–2). A light from heaven suddenly flashed around him. He fell to the ground and heard a voice say to him, "Saul, Saul, why are you persecuting Me?"(9:4). "Who are you, Lord?" he inquired. "I am Jesus, whom you are persecuting . . ." the voice responded. "Arise and go into the city, and you will be told what you must do" (Acts 9:6). His life would never be the same.

Once in the forefront of persecuting those of the Way, Paul became their most tireless advocate. From his perspective, he was ". . . the least of the apostles, who am not worthy to be called an apostle, because I persecuted the church of God. But by the grace of God I am what I am, and His grace toward me was not in vain; but I labored more abundantly than they all, yet not I, but the grace of God which was with me" (1 Corinthians 15:9, 10).

Paul bequeathed to us a far more extensive collection of literature than any of the other apostolic missions. In particular, we have his addresses in Acts, and his extensive correspondence. The most substantive of Paul's addresses were delivered in the Pisidian Antioch synagogue (Acts 13:16–41), and before the Athenian Areopagus, its highest court (17:22–31). As the apostle to the Gentiles, Paul preserved the usual apostolic practice of preaching in synagogues, especially when entering a new mission city. What he preached, however, was vintage Pauline doctrines of grace without compromise to the Judaizers who pressed for more obeisance to Moses by Gentile converts. His passion and direct approach in the synagogues accounted for many of the stripes and threatened stonings Paul suffered over the years.

But before Paul began his extensive travels and work among the Gentiles, he lived as a tentmaker in his hometown of Tarsus for more than ten years. Although he was unafraid to confess Jesus and his new birth before all (9:20–22, 26–29), during this time he mostly prepared himself with study, prayers, fasting, and further mentoring by the church elders of Damascus, Antioch, and Jerusalem.

On one particular Sabbath in Damascus, Paul stood in the synagogue and captured the attention of all present with a long rehearsal of Israel's historical promises of God. He declared "... that promise which was made to the fathers. God has fulfilled this for us their children, in that He has raised up Jesus" (Acts 13:32–33). This message was well received by the congregation, and a large crowd gathered the following Sabbath to hear Paul again. This success was the beginning of Paul's troubles with resistance and persecution from the prominent people of the cities where he labored (13:45 and 50).

As elsewhere, Paul lost much of his audience in that Damascus synagogue by bringing in the themes of sin, repentance, and the salvation mission of Christ. However, some indicated that they would like to hear more from Paul concerning these matters, and a few even believed. These two speeches, however, along with the background information about Paul's life, set a foundation for understanding Paul's teaching of the gospel message as illustrated by his work and his writings.

Paul's Teachings about the Gospel

"Moreover brethren," Paul writes, "I declare to you the gospel which I preached to you . . ." (1 Corinthians 15:1–8).

"For I delivered to you first of all that which I also received; that Christ died for our sins according to the Scriptures, that He was buried, and that He rose again the third day according to the Scriptures, and that He was seen by Cephas then by the twelve. After that He was seen by over five hundred brethren at once, of whom the greater part remain to the present . . ." (15:3–6). Then, last of all, He appeared to Paul.

He "died for our sins"; that is, he atoned for our sins. It was "according to the Scriptures"; as such, it was in keeping with God's providential plan from the beginning of creation (Ephesians 1:4; Revelation 13:8). He "was buried"; he actually died. "He rose again"; Christian faith consists of resurrection faith. Believers must be convinced that Jesus was raised from the dead. That is the core of Christian faith. Paul pointed to the Cross, to the tomb, to the resurrected, flesh and blood body of Jesus, and to the hope of glory for all who know Him as Savior. This testimony of substantial faith, which is equally significant and redemptive in the spiritual as well as the physical realm, was a profound challenge in the Hellenistic and pagan culture in which Paul traveled. It is also, incidentally, a direct contradiction of a minority of Paul's radical detractors who argued that his doctrine was alien to the Jerusalem church and the other apostles, and merely a repackaged version of Mithraism and other pagan mystery religions. But this controversy has already been laid to rest in more scholarly explorations of Paul's theology.

The implication for those who believe is that the followers of Jesus are identified with Him in His death and Resurrection. Paul continued: "Therefore we were buried with Him through baptism into death, that just as Christ was raised from the dead by the glory of the Father, even so we also should walk in newness of life" (Romans 6:4). "For as in Adam all die, even so in Christ all shall be made alive. But each one in his own order: Christ the firstfruits, afterward those who are Christ's at His coming" (1 Corinthians 15:22–23).

Paul sees Christ as the central figure in this history of salvation. He stands where we cannot, and He stands there at the Cross for us. "For there is one God," Paul assures us, "and one Mediator between God and men, the Man Christ Jesus, who gave Himself as a ransom for all . . ." (1 Timothy 2:5–6).

It is because of Christ's ransoming of all mankind that believers are forever changed by their acceptance of Him. "Therefore, if anyone is in Christ, he is a new creation; old things have passed away; behold, all things have become new. Now all things are of God, who has reconciled us to Himself through Jesus Christ, and has given us the ministry of reconciliation, that is, that God was in Christ reconciling the world to Himself, not imputing their trespasses to them, and has commited to us the word of reconciliation" (2 Corinthians 5:17–19).

Paul continued by pointing out that, "Stand fast therefore in the liberty by which Christ has made us free, and do not be entangled again with a yoke of bondage" (Galatians 5:1). That involves freedom from bondage to sin, freedom to mature in Christ, and freedom for God's service, and a ministry to others. Another change brought to the believer is a justification before God: "Who was delivered up because of our offenses, and was raised because of our justification" (Romans 4:25). Thus, in Paul's view, believers are acquitted of all sins because Jesus died and was resurrected.

Likewise, as all believers are equally freed from the consequences of sin, they are alike in the eyes of God in other ways, as well. Sin impacted each one equally (3:22–23), and God's forgiveness, as well as a unity with Christ in faith, brings every believer to the table at the same time, to share in the freedom God has given them.

> Paul was martyred sometime near the end of Nero's rule.
>
> —*Legend*

The phrase "in Christ" occurs with some variation approximately 165 times in Paul's epistles. For instance, "Therefore, if anyone is in Christ, he is a new creation; old things have passed away; behold, all things have become new" (2 Corinthians 5:17). So Paul reminded his readers to "put off, concerning your former conduct, the old man which grows corrupt according to the deceitful lusts, and be renewed in the spirit of your mind, and that you put on the new man which was created according to God, in true righteousness and holiness" (Ephesians 4:22–24). This would seem to imply a symbiotic union between Christ and the believer. With such in mind, Paul confidently affirmed: "I can do all things through Christ who strengthens me" (Philippians 4:13).

This unity in Christ, however, does not mean that following Christ is an easy journey. The demands and disciplines of the Christian life involve sacrifice, devotion, and sometimes just plain, hard work. "I beseech you therefore, brethren, by the mercies of God, that you present your bodies a living sacrifice, holy, acceptable to God, which is your reasonable service" (Romans 12:1).

It remains entirely uncertain who wrote the epistle to the Hebrews. Some scholars believe from its style that it was Paul himself or one of his associates with his oversight. Most scholars, however, seem reluctant about debating any definite authorship for Hebrews. To them the issue is and should remain a mystery until the unlikely appearance of some compelling evidence favoring a particular author.

Nevertheless, the following exhortations from the final chapters of Hebrews are certainly Pauline in their declarative style and pastoral character. Indeed, they highlight the spirit and purpose that captivated the hearts and lives of the other apostles of the good news. Hebrews is authored in the spirit of grace that encourages us all regarding the ministry of reconciling the world to Christ.

"Therefore, brethren, having boldness to enter the Holiest by the blood of Jesus, by a new and living way which He consecrated for us, through the veil, that is, His flesh, and having a High Priest over the house of God, let us draw near with a true heart in full assurance of faith, having our hearts sprinkled from an evil conscience and our bodies washed with pure water. Let us hold fast the confession of our hope without wavering, for He who promised is faithful. And let us consider one another in order to stir up love and good works, not forsaking the assembling of ourselves together, as is the manner of some, but exhorting one another, and so much the more as you see the Day approaching" (Hebrews 10:19–25).

"Now faith is the substance of things hoped for, the evidence of things not seen. For by it the elders obtained a good testimony" (11:1–2).

Paul may have died on the same day and at the same time as the apostle Peter.

—*Legend*

"Therefore we also, since we are surrounded by so great a cloud of witnesses, let us lay aside every weight, and the sin which so easily ensnares us, and let us run with endurance the race that is set before us, looking unto Jesus, the author and finisher of our faith, who for the joy that was set before Him endured the cross, despising the shame, and has sat down at the right hand of the throne of God" (Hebrews 12:1–2).

"Pray for us . . . Now may the God of peace who brought up our Lord Jesus from the dead, that great Shepherd of the sheep, through the blood of the everlasting covenant, make you complete in every good work to do His will, working in you what is well pleasing in His sight, through Jesus Christ, to whom be glory forever and ever. Amen" (13:18, 20–21).

Apostolic Symbols and Patronages of Paul

The apostolic symbols for Paul are a man holding a sword and a book, a man with three springs of water, a sword, or a book. He is usually depicted as a thin, elderly man with a long beard and a receding hairline.

Paul's patronage has been linked to:

- Authors, writers, and journalists
- Evangelists
- Diocese of Birmingham, AL, Covington, KY, Las Vegas, NV, Providence, RI, Worcester, MS
- Hailstorms
- Public relations workers
- Malta
- Musicians
- Rope braiders/makers
- Saddlers/saddle makers
- Snake bite victims/against snakes
- Tentmakers

Memorials

25 January (Paul's conversion)
29 June (Peter and Paul as co-founders of the Church)
18 November (Feast of the Dedication of the Basilicas of Peter and Paul)

Where to Find Paul in the Bible[9]

From birth to conversion:

Ω Acts 22:3	Born at Tarsus in Cilicia
Ω Acts 22:25–28	Born a Roman citizen
Ω Acts 9:11, Acts 13:9	Called Saul until changed to Paul
Ω Philippians 3:5	Benjamite Jew
Ω Acts 21:39	Citizen of Tarsus
Ω Acts 18:3	By trade a tentmaker
Ω Acts 26:4–5, Gal. 1:14	Zealot for Judaism
Ω Acts 23:6, Philippians 3:5, 6	Very strict Pharisee
Ω Acts 22:3	Educated under Gamaliel

Ω Acts 23:16	His sister in Jerusalem
Ω 1 Corinthians 9:5	Apparently unmarried
Ω Acts 26:10	Member of council
Ω Acts 7:58, Acts 8:1, Acts 22:20	Consented to Stephen's death
Ω Acts 9:1, 2, Acts 22:3–5, Acts 26:10, 11, Galatians 1:13	Intensified persecution of Christians
Ω Acts 26:9, 1 Timothy 1:13	Blasphemous and violent persecutor

His conversion:

Ω Acts 9:3–9	On road to Damascus
Ω Acts 9:6, 10–18, Ephesians 3:1–8	Given a commission
Ω Acts 9:6, 10–18	Instructed and baptized by Ananias
Ω Acts 22:1–16, Acts 26:1–20	Repeated his conversion story
Ω 1 Corinthians 9:1, 16, 1 Corinthians 15:8–10, Galatians 1:12–16	Referred to it often
Ω Ephesians 3:1–8	Considered himself unworthy
Ω 1 Timothy 1:12–16	Regretted former life
Ω Romans 1:16, 2 Timothy 1:8–12	Not ashamed of Christ
Ω Acts 9:19–22	Preached Jesus as Christ (Messiah)
Ω Acts 9:23–25, 2 Corinthians 11:32	Persecuted by Jews
Ω Galatians 1:17–19	Met and visited Peter

Ω Acts 22:17–21	Received vision of his ministry to Gentiles
Ω Acts 9:29, 30, Galatians 1:21	Sent to Tarsus
Ω Acts 11:22–26	Brought to Antioch (in Syria) by Barnabas
Ω Acts 11:27–30	Sent to Jerusalem with relief
Ω Acts 12:25	Returned to Antioch
Ω Acts 15:2–22, Galatians 2:1–10	Participated in Jerusalem Council
Ω Galatians 2:11–21	Rebuked Peter in Antioch

Missionary Journeys:

Ω Acts 13:1—14:26	First missionary journey
Ω Acts 15—18:22	Second missionary journey
Ω Acts 18:23—21:8	Third missionary journey

In Jerusalem and Caesarea:

Ω Acts 21:15—26:32	Arrived in Jerusalem; welcomed by church; Plotted against and falsely accused, arrest and appeal to Caesar
Ω Acts 27—28	Sailing under arrest to Rome
Ω Acts 28:3–5	Bitten by poisonous snake but unharmed

Final ministry and death:

Ω 2 Timothy 4:20	Visited Macedonia and other places
Ω 2 Timothy 1:8, 2 Timothy 4:6–8	Wrote Second Timothy from Roman prison
Ω 2 Timothy 4:9–22	Sent final news and greetings

Characteristics of Paul:

Ω 1 Corinthians 4:1–15, Philippians 3:7–14	Consecrated
Ω Acts 16:25, 2 Corinthians 4:8–10	Cheerful
Ω Acts 9:29, Acts 20:22–24	Courageous
Ω Philippians 2:25–30, Philemon 7–24	Considerate of others
Ω 2 Corinthians 1:12–17, 2 Corinthians 6:3, 4	Conscientious
Ω 2 Corinthians 4:10, 11, Philippians 1:20–23	Christ-centered
Ω 2 Corinthians 2:1–11, Galatians 2:1–15	Conciliatory
Ω 2 Corinthians 12:8–10, 2 Timothy 4:7, 8	Composed

Endnotes

1. Lane, William. *The Gospel According to Mark.* Grand Rapids: Eerdmans, 1974.
2. Lactantius, *On the Manner in Which the Persecutors Died.* II.
3. *Acts of Peter and Andrew.*
4. Whyte, Alexander. *Bible Characters from the Old and New Testaments.* Pentecostal Publishing Company, 1990.
5. Goodspeed, Edgar, J. *The Twelve: The Story of Christ's Apostles.* Philadelphia: J. C. Winston, 1957.
6. Jowett, George, F. *The Drama of the Lost Disciples.* London: Covenant Publishing Company, 1970.
7. Peter of Alexandria. *The Canonical Epistle.*
8. Newman, Dorman. *The Lives and Deaths of the Holy Apostles.* London: Kings Arms in the Poultry, 1685.
9. Thomas Nelson, Inc. *Nelson's Quick Reference Topical Bible Index.* Nashville: Thomas Nelson, Inc., 1995.
10. Inch, Morris. *Exhortations of Jesus According to Matthew* and *Up From the Depths: Mark as Tragedy.* Lanham: University Press of America, 1997.
11. Hagner, Donald. *Matthew 14—28.* Dallas: Word, 1995.
12. Hurtado, Larry. *Mark.* Peabody: Hendrickson, 1983.
13. Sharp, Mary. *A Traveler's Guide to Saints in Europe.* London: Trinity Press, 1964.
14. Bauman, Richard. *Story, Performance and Event: Contextual Stories in Oral Tradition.* Cambridge: Cambridge University, 1987.

Jesus called them one by one,
Peter, Andrew, James and John,
Philip and Bartholomew,
Doubting Thomas and Matthew.

Chorus
Yes, Jesus called them,
Yes, Jesus called them,
Yes, Jesus called them,
He called them one by one.

James the one they called the less,
Simon, also Thaddaeus
The twelfth apostle Judas made,
Jesus was by him betrayed.

Chorus
Yes, Jesus called them,
Yes, Jesus called them,
Yes, Jesus called them,
He called them one by one.